RISE UP

The Blueprint For Manager Success

10 Keys To Getting Things Done

Visionary Author
Cedrick LaFleur

LaFleur Leadership Institute
www.lafleurleadershipinstitute.com
Cedrick.lafleur2@gmail.com

ISBN: 9798432782816

Ordering Information:
Quantity Sales- Special discounts are available on quantity purchases by corporations, associations, and nonprofits. For details contact the publisher at the address above.

Edited and Formatted By: Trendy Elite Media Group and Published by Cedrick LaFleur.

This book is intended to provide personal growth and leadership strategies that will assist the reader in their journey to developing the strong leadership and interpersonal skills needed to feel confident and lead fearlessly inside and outside of the workplace. This book is not intended to provide financial, emotional health, or legal advice. Please seek appropriate counsel for financial, emotional health, or legal matters.

EXECUTIVE SUMMARY

Management must be effective for the success of any business. Unfortunately, it is all too easy to overlook the training and development of new managers. When you provide your managers and employees with the skills and tools they need, you will greatly boost morale and strengthen your organization. With this book **Rise Up: The Blueprint for Manager Success,** you will understand the value of investing in employees and developing management. By focusing on development opportunities, you will establish a culture that retains top talent and improves succession planning.

TABLE OF CONTENTS

FOREWORD

As an entrepreneur, business leader and international speaker, trainer, and high-performance coach for the past three decades, one thing I have learned is that top companies and teams do consistently; they invest in the development of their people.

Although it may seem common sense to do so, we have all heard the saying that common sense isn't always so common.

Investing in your people requires the leadership to have a long-term focus on their business and their people. It requires that they play the long game in a world that focuses on the short game, quick fixes, and immediate results.

Of course, anyone who has built a meaningful, sustainable business knows the pitfalls of the short game, quick fixes, and seeking immediate results, they are just that, short fixes that produce an immediate result. But rarely the results we hope for the long haul.

At the time I am writing this foreword, Microsoft is a 46-year-old company, I know it's hard for some Gen X'ers to believe that this company we grew up on has been around nearly all of our lives, but it has. From the looks of things today, with the stock price at an all-time high and the future as bright as ever, it looks like it will likely outlive all of us!

The question is, what contributed to its success?

Well, we know since its inception, its founder and original CEO Bill Gates was insistent that the team at Microsoft be the smartest and best-equipped people.

Early on he put in place training and development programs for every employee within the company, a sort of growth plan for them personally and professionally throughout the ranks of the company.

These investments paid off huge, giving Microsoft a deep bench of talent and a loyal and motivated team. It also built a culture of lifelong learning.

Bill gates was asked in an interview in the 1980's "What keeps you up at night," and he famously said it was that some 14-year old kid was sitting in his mom and dad's garage plotting the demise of Microsoft!

He didn't mean there was some sinister plot to hurt him or the people; he meant that some kid was in their garage learning not just the cutting-edge knowledge but the bleeding edge knowledge of what will be the future. Gates knew he needed to invest in his peoples' growth and learning, and not just in their trade skills. Invest in soft interpersonal skills like goal setting, communication, leadership, vision building, conflict resolution, and even sales. Skills that if not developed, often lead to failure.

At a time when very few companies in his industry were investing in their people, Gates was almost fanatical about it. He was and still is a committed lifelong learner.

What are the results of this commitment to personal growth and team development?

Well, it's having exactly what I said earlier, a meaningful, sustainable business.

Microsoft grew to be one of the first trillion-dollar companies.

It's been around for more than four decades. Gates has been gone from that company for a third of that time, retiring over 17 years ago, Yet, the company stands today as arguably one of the most relevant companies of our time.

People matter; period. People make or break a business, an organization, or a movement.

Without question, the very best way to predict a future outcome is to evaluate the growth path of the people involved. If the people inside the four walls don't grow, the business won't grow, no matter how good the product, market, or opportunity.

Studies today have also shown that the very best people will not stay in an environment where they are not growing. If the company doesn't invest in them, they leave, and they take the second-tier talent with them, leaving the short-sighted, quick-fix, short-game players who were chasing immediate results, to manage a business that is dying from the inside out.

The formula for the personal growth of team members is not complicated or even expensive to implement, it's certainly a lot less costly than having a team that isn't committed to growth, and this process is outlined in the pages of this book.

Coaching, mentorship, targeted skill training workshops, and a measured personal growth plan are key components to a well-rounded program that fosters growth and development and brings out the best in people.

Foreword

As a provider for these types of services, I and the contributors of this book are often asked a question by HR leaders, CEOs, and key financial decision makers within a company. The question is this:

"What if we invest all this time and money in our people, and they leave?"

Well, that's a fair question and a real possibility, no doubt about it.

I think a better question is this:

"What if you don't invest in all these people's growth and development, and they stay?"

What will happen to your company if your team's best and most creative thinking happened yesterday, or last quarter or last year? What if this is as good as it gets?

What's the cost of having a project be slow-played or worse because your team doesn't know how to communicate effectively with each other?

What's the cost of poor leadership?

What's the cost of hunting new talent because your people haven't grown and developed?

I think intuitively, you know the answers to these questions, and they don't paint a pretty picture of the future.

In this book, you will learn how people learn and grow, how to create a culture of lifelong learning, and how to map out a personal growth plan for yourself and everyone on your team.

I'd encourage you to investigate the possibilities of how you can implement a growth plan within your business or organization by speaking to one of this book's contributors.

One of my favorite quotes is by Eric Hoffer, and I think it makes a case for growth and development for all of us. He said:

"In times of change, learners inherit the earth, while the learned find themselves beautifully equipped to deal with a world that no longer exists."

You have a choice today to be one of those learners, who fosters the growth and learning in yourself and others, don't be short-sighted, don't chase the quick fix or the fast short-lived result. Invest in yourself and your people, play the long game, and win forever.

Paul Martinelli

CHAPTER 1

YOU CAN DO THIS TOO

Today is the day! You arrive at the office of your new employer. Nothing and no one is truly familiar to you; after all, it's just your first day. You're already the new kid on the block, and deep down inside, you *really* don't know what that means, except for the fact that this is your first day of employment.

Certainly, no one is referring to the American boy band from the late '80s.

While you are engaged in your grand tour around the office, you notice a very large corner office. This is not just any office, but it is a well-furnished office encased in glass, with an amazing outside view. Immediately, you say to yourself, "one day, this will be my office." You're not sure what it's going to take for you to get into an office like that just yet. All you know is that you set your sights on becoming more on that day.

"More" is a great sight! No one wants to remain in the same seat year after year after year without the opportunity to advance. However, there are steps to advancement, especially managerial advancement, that is the responsibility of both the aspiring candidate and the organization.

Now allow me to stop you right here because I can hear your sigh. You feel that, although advancement to Managerial Leadership is your desire, you just don't have what it takes to get there, and you're simply not qualified. Well, hold your image; I have great news for you... Managers are made, not born! Yes, you read that correctly. Managers are made, not born.

You Don't Have to Know It All...Initially!

Effective management is a skill. It's a set of skills that can be learned. It requires the willingness on behalf of the employer to invest in its employees, especially those who aspire to one day be in leadership. It requires the desire of the employee to take advantage of the opportunities to learn and develop those skills.

Effective management does not necessarily require an associate, bachelor, a MBA, or a Ph.D. in Management, Business, or Leadership.

While these earnings are never wasteful, they are evidence of the new managers' disciplines and intentions to be the best in their industry and for their organization.

Allow me to get personal for just a second.

Because I am aware that management is leadership, excuse me if I use both words interchangeably and maybe even together. I have been in leadership and management for quite some time, in a myriad of industries, from religious institutions to real estate. Good leaders and managers are necessary for every industry. I have served in county government offices, residential real estate, commercial real estate, in addition to religious organizations, and I have held and currently hold leadership positions in each of those entities.

I was a teenage mom who initially did not take advantage of the opportunity to complete my aspiring concentration in business administration and management. Instead, I bought into the narrative that I had become a waste, and everything that I'd dreamed of becoming and desired to do was washed away.

Having become a mother as a teenager, I thought that there was nothing available for me except a government system handout, for which I should have been very grateful.

Initially, I accepted that narrative until, one day, I realized that I had settled but was destined for more. After several years of being a system recipient, I decided to work. I had no skills other than typing at a rapid pace, which I learned while in High School.

I had nothing but a high school diploma and a few college credits.

As I entered the workforce, to the surprise of some, I could galvanize groups and cause them to buy into projects because I am a natural communicator and influencer. Although I had a talent for people, we all learned quickly that talent just wasn't enough. Talent is a person's innate or natural ability to do something, while skill is an ability garnered through training and practice. With each opportunity, I worked very hard. Still, I had several lessons yet to realize to become an effective manager and leader.

I took the word BOSS literally. I am sure that those who worked with me would never say this, but I was kind of a tyrant. I was a micro-manager, so I could not get the best from my team. In addition, I didn't know how to identify the abilities of my team members and foster their individual growth. Now mind you, yes, I was friendly, but not balanced. I was your homegirl, but I lacked specific necessary skills. I became a body in a seat without the required influence to grow those around me.

Managers Are Made, Not Born

As I previously stated, there are needed skills to succeed in management. While the list below is not exhaustive, among them are:

- Effective Communication
- Time Management
- People Management
- Interpersonal Skills
- Decision Making & Delegation Skills

These and other skill sets are developed through time, effort, discipline, and desire. New Managers learn by watching, doing, and most importantly, being managed well. In your career, you will have the opportunity to encounter various types of managers. Some will only care about the production rather than the person.

Guard yourself against becoming that type of manager. Remember this...*people matter*!

Take the time to study your industry, more specifically, your organization. Do not be afraid to learn the various job functions. You are being immersed in a new world and learning as much as possible will assist you in your role as a manager and leader. Learn each process and procedure. Become as knowledgeable as possible to serve as a resource to those around you.

As you grow from team member to manager, remember that it is acceptable to ask the team for assistance. Even though you're the manager, remember the adage that says it's the "teamwork that makes the dream work". Although you are leading the team, you are still a part of the team.

You are managing processes, and you are managing people, and you need the people to get the work done. It would help if you became acquainted with each team member's bandwidth.

The ability to understand this is huge.

Knowing this will help you minimize the frustration of the individuals on the team as well as yourself. This will also aid you in understanding how to support your team members and champion them towards their own success.

Once you understand each member's bandwidth, now you must learn how everyone receives and processes information. This is the hidden gem! It's the value of effective communication. Nothing can destroy a team faster than a manager with ineffective communication skills.

In the book "Everyone, Communicates, Few Connect" by John Maxwell, John states that effective communication requires a connection. He asserts that **"connecting is the ability to identify with people and relate to them in a way that increases your influence with them."**

I would insert here that communication is more about listening and connecting versus speaking. You must learn to tune in to people's pain points, whether personal or professional. The most successful way to do this is to listen to them.

Your career journey will have good and bad experiences, but each experience will shape your success as a leader.

Of course, when you join an organization, your prior experience may not necessarily be the full fit for rapid movement; however, as you grow in your position, you may build a foundation that can eventually guarantee your career promotion.

What's Next?

I want to take a minute to encourage you to get and stay **F-A-T!** I learned this while reading Howard Hendrick's book titled "Living by the Book".

- Remain **F**aithful
- Remain **A**vailable
- Remain **T**eachable

I will add (2) additional thoughts to this:

- Stay Hungry
- Stay Humble

In conclusion, find a mentor inside of your organization as well outside of your organization. A mentor will help enhance your self-awareness and assist you in maintaining a balance. You may also invest in a coach, purchase a few books, or even take a few courses. In addition, you may find certifications that will also aid in your success. Finally, check with your employer to see what they may offer in a reimbursement program. Whatever you do, remember that *YOUR* personal growth & development is paramount to your next level.

CONGRATULATIONS! You've got this!

CHAPTER 2

FOUR CRITICAL ELEMENTS TO A WELL-DEFINED MANAGEMENT ROADMAP

"Leaders are made; they are not born. They are made by hard effort" — Vince Lombardi

Early in my career after I graduated with my bachelor's degree in clinical laboratory sciences and had worked for a local hospital for a few years, I was ready to take on a management role in my department. I had no idea what steps to take to position myself for an opportunity when it became available. To me, it seemed like everyone else was moving up the corporate ladder with ease, but I couldn't figure out how it was happening. It wasn't until I spoke with another colleague that I learned of the management roadmap that my hospital had for aspiring future supervisors and managers.

Does your organization have an established roadmap or career ladder for employees to move into management positions? If so, do you know how to access it? A roadmap is essential to your career success, and a defined management roadmap is vital for organizational success. The management roadmap provides employees who want to assume higher levels of authority with a guide. The guide covers the competencies, skills, and professional development they will need to become effective managers and leaders.

The importance of understanding four critical elements of a well-defined management roadmap is covered in this chapter.

These elements include:

- Clearly defined roles and competencies
- Tools managers need to be successful
- Identification of candidates for the management pipeline
- Creation of a management track

Here you will receive an overview of the core essence of developing a new manager and leader. Each subsequent chapter will dive into these topics in greater detail.

Roles and Competencies Must Be Clearly Defined

Defining roles and competencies in an organization is like defining the pieces of a puzzle. To have all the pieces for solving a puzzle, you need to know what each piece looks like and what it does. It is essential to define what managers do and their skills and competencies to manage successfully. Having a clear vision and understanding of the core aspects of the role before stepping into the job will also add to your success.

Roles of Managers

The first step in creating a management roadmap is defining what managers do and what skills and competencies they need to manage successfully. This can be done through a formal process, but it is also possible to clarify these things informally. A traditional way to understand manager requirements is to look at current job descriptions and see the requirements and duties. An informal way would be to briefly interview current managers and leaders on what it is like to walk a day in their shoes. This will help to understand better some of the things not listed in the job description. Based on these observations, a list of core competencies managers need to succeed can be created. Don't underestimate interviewing front-line staff on their expectations to see if it aligns with what managers do and their responsibilities.

Required Competencies

Measuring the competencies of managers is essential for performance reviews, professional development planning, and workplace accountability. Competencies are skills that define what an employee needs to do their job well. Each competency should be measurable so that employee progress can be tracked. It may be necessary to work with managers to develop and implement a process for identifying gaps in competencies as required by their current or future leadership role. One way to measure progress is to track the number of times a skill is used on the job or in training sessions. Another option is to use an assessment tool such as DISC or Myers-Briggs to measure knowledge, skills, behavior, and abilities.

Below are six critical competencies of effective managers:

- Effective communication
- Delegation
- Prioritization
- Networking
- Time Management

- Emotional Intelligence

By evaluating managers based on objective measurements of their performance, they can be more easily rewarded for their successes or coached when they are struggling.

The Manager's Toolkit

"Good managers are teachers, coaches, and friends. They teach their employees what they need to know to do their jobs well; coach them on how to get better and provide emotional support when they're struggling."
— *Coach Tee Wilson*

It is vital to provide new managers and employees with management potential the tools they need to become effective managers. Just like you can't teach someone to ride a bike without giving them the bike to ride, you cannot teach someone to be an effective manager without giving them the tools needed to become one. Even the most motivated and passionate new manager will struggle if not given the tools necessary to succeed. Therefore, managers need to have a variety of tools in their toolkits.

Tools and resources that I have found to be of value on my leadership journey include:

- Formal and informal mentorship
- Web resources
- External development opportunities
- Peer groups for additional support
- Technology how-to guides
- Coaching to increase visibility and
- Meeting templates
- Performance management tools

- Phone list of key contacts
- Time management calculators
- Scheduling tools
- Project management software
- Electronic note-taking apps

In addition to the tools mentioned above, ask current managers what they find valuable. Don't forget to ensure that new and future managers know these tools and how to access them.

The Selection Process: Identifying Candidates Early

It's no secret that the pool of competent and confident managers is declining, and soon there will be a gap. If you're unprepared for this gap, your organization will be in trouble. One way to prepare for this gap is by identifying future management talent as early as possible. Essentially, you have to find a diamond in the rough and cut it. This practice gives you the best chance to develop successful managers who can help lead your organization into the next generation.

Identifying candidates for the management track as early as possible gives you the best chance to develop successful managers. It provides employees with the skills, experiences, and professional development they need to become industry-ready professionals. The earlier an employee can begin building the competencies they will need in a managerial role, the more likely they will be successful. Similarly, identifying management candidates earlier allows you to pair these employees with mentors to help them navigate the management track and access the necessary tools and training. Having management candidates in the pipeline is helpful in succession planning. It is beneficial to talk to employees about their long-term career plans to identify potential management candidates early. Discussions can happen in informal meetings during reviews or huddle discussions. Current managers and supervisors can also recommend employees they think show potential for the management pipeline.

When looking for aspiring managers, the best way to spot management potential is to notice how they interact with peers and communicate with team members. For example, are there any informal leaders in your department? Start by looking at how they handle conflict with peers. If they always respectfully resolve things; or serve as the go-to person for their coworkers, then they have what it takes to be a good manager.

Create A Management Track

"Organizations are more complex than ever been before. The best way to manage them is to understand what strategies will work best for each."
— *Tywauna Wilson*

Your job is like a train. You need to ensure everyone is on the same page to get to your destination. Creating a management track is vital for all employees to grasp. Creating a management track needs to be crystal-clear to all employees. Setting up a clear management track is an invaluable tool in developing managers. A clear management track means providing individuals with enough opportunity to learn, grow, and demonstrate their skills. So they can get the most out of the time spent on the job. Sometimes this may require additional training or coaching to make all future transitions easier for the employees, reduce the stress and overwhelm, and create a happier workforce.

Organizations looking to establish a clear management track can do so by focusing on the following five areas:

1. Organizing one's work in a way that makes management seem like the next logical step in career progression
2. Enhancing one's managerial skills
3. Gaining knowledge in management techniques
4. Understanding the company culture and building relationships with coworkers
5. Understanding their strengths

These key areas enable leaders to self-assess their current capabilities and insights and the experiences and professional development training that can help them advance into management positions.

Employees must know that the management track exists! A well-defined management track empowers employees to grow towards managerial positions. When identifying management candidates, discuss the potential with the employee and let them know how to access the management track information. You can provide material outlining the management track or make these materials available electronically via your company intranet.

In conclusion, a well-defined management roadmap with clearly defined roles and competencies and the proper tools can help managers and future leaders navigate successfully. It is crucial to have a clear, well-defined plan that breaks the process into manageable sections to successfully acclimate to a new management role or transition from peer to lead. A clear, well-defined management roadmap will help the organization stay on track and reassure employees that they are not being left behind in the process.

Practical Illustration

In Ohio, a small community hospital recently saw many of its tenured staff retiring with no candidates in the pipeline to assume the vacant management roles. A committee was formed to examine why few candidates were ready for promotion to these roles, which caused major succession planning issues. The committee began to interview employees throughout the organization. The interviews began with its current management team and then engaged top performers, tenured team members, and even newer employees who had been with the organization for six months or less. After talking with many team members, the feedback was consistent and is summarized below:

- Managers didn't know the expectations of their new role
- Front line team members didn't know how they could move into management roles
- It was unclear which of the actual competencies were needed to succeed in management
- There were no internal leadership development programs
- There was limited feedback available to the staff
- No established formal mentoring of front-line staff or managers, so they often lack direction and clarity.

The committee came up with recommendations to create a management roadmap so that employees were clear on the steps to transition from peer to lead. This roadmap consisted of a leadership development program to help managers and future managers develop the competencies and skills to be effective in leadership roles. They also recommended that current managers analyze their respective teams and identify those employees who have management potential and aspire to be in leadership. Within a year of implementing some of the committee's ideas, the organization began seeing more internal candidates apply for management roles as they become available and other candidates in the pipeline.

CHAPTER 3

DEFINE AND BUILD COMPETENCIES

"The growth and development of people is the highest calling of leadership." — Harvey Firestone

The skills for effective management can be learned and built. However, they can only be understood and built if those who aspire to leadership know what those skills and competencies are. When you take the time to define the core competencies needed for management then create opportunities to build and practice those competencies, it is a valuable investment in developing new managers. Incorporating these clearly defined competencies into the management track is also vital.

The organization must be willing to take the first steps in developing its people. The organization should provide the necessary tools, classes, and availability to make the program effective. In other words, it should be a top-down approach to developing people.

Once the organization makes the program available, the ownership switches to the employee, growth will not automatically happen, and each person must take specific, intentional actions to grow.

"An investment in your personal development is the best investment you can make." — Jim Rohn

During my time in corporate leadership, I had one annual requirement for every team member. Each person was required to enroll in at least one developmental course yearly, and the organization would cover the cost. It was not optional; it was the standard. I so strongly believed in personal growth and development that I wanted to ensure our people were on a continuous growth journey. Each person was responsible for deciding which course they wanted to take and when they would take it. We would then set up a time to review and approve the path forward.

In this chapter, you will gain some of the insights I used to help my team members grow and develop. Leaders must constantly and consistently ask themselves:

- What am I doing to develop my potential as a leader?
- Am I assisting other leaders in developing their potential?

Asking questions will lead you in the right direction for empowering people and successful leadership.

Without this insight, you will find yourself disconnected from your employees.

Clearly Define Competencies Needed

What does it take to be an effective manager? What does it take to be an effective leader? These are essential questions that go unasked far too often. When creating a more transparent management track and plan for developing new managers, take a step back and ask what competencies and skills effective managers/leaders practice: interview managers, supervisors, and frontline employees. Ask managers about their workday, the challenges they face, and the tools they use.

I have interviewed over 100 leaders from different size organizations with varying experience levels; Corporate Presidents, Vice Presidents, Director level, front line employees, and solo entrepreneurs to find out what skills/strengths they believe good leaders should possess.

Below are the Top 25 skills that successful managers/leaders possess:

- Humility
- Integrity
- Honesty
- Compassion
- Be a lifelong learner
- Be Authentic
- Be Empathetic
- Create a foundation of trust
- Understand each person individually
- Be flexible with each person
- Be technically competent
- Be a great communicator the higher you go
- Be able to make tough decisions but be fair at the same time
- Detail-oriented
- Be vulnerable
- Share stories
- Be a good communicator
- See your people as people
- Active listener
- Self-awareness (Emotional Intelligence)
- Ability to delegate
- Be a Visionary
- Invest in People

- Serve Others
- Resilience

This list is not exhaustive; however, it does show you that to become an effective leader, you must be intentional, flexible, and willing to develop yourself.

You can also look to best practices in other organizations or divisions. Using the list of roles and competencies you created when you defined the management track is also a good idea. You will create a clear, concise list of the competencies managers need to succeed in your organization. These competencies must be *specific, measurable, attainable, realistic, and timely* (SMART) both so employees can evaluate themselves and supervisors can evaluate new managers and provide them with feedback.

The journey to becoming a good leader should directly correlate to your success journey. As you embark on your success journey, you must define what it takes to succeed. Many people have the wrong description. They think that success comes in the form of money, power, achievements, or possessions; others believe that success is the pursuit of happiness, though their quest for it makes them continually miserable. Success is not a destination; it is a process. Success comes from having a mission in life and knowing how to grow to fulfill it. You must be willing to go deep within yourself to become an effective and successful leader. Leader guru John C. Maxwell states that "Everything rises and falls on leadership." If that is the case, that means you must be willing to grow others.

Identify Strengths

Every employee has some things they do well. When working with new managers or those on the management track, first identify an individual's strengths. An effective strategy is to ask the employee to list their areas of strength and ask supervisors or peers to (anonymously) list that employee's strengths. Use your evaluation of the employee as well. By identifying the employee's strengths, you can find areas in which they already demonstrate key competencies or areas in which his strengths are used to build those competencies. The process of identifying strengths may also be part of your overall process of identifying management candidates.

Marcus Buckingham asked in his book, Go Put Your Strengths to Work, "*Did you know that only 17% of people feel they spend the majority of their work playing to their strengths? That means only 2 out of 10 people put their strengths to work every day! Are you one of them?*".

The key to identifying strengths is to ask a lot of questions. When you ask good questions, you help bring out the best in a person.

Too often, we tell people what they are good at instead of asking them what they believe they are good at doing.

When you understand you are on the same page with an employee, you can lead them better. This leading is also known as consensus building with your employee.

One of the greatest college basketball coaches of all time is the Six-time National Champion Pat Summit. Coach Summit is the all-time winningness coach at the University of Tennessee.

Coach Summit explained that the players would go into the dressing room at halftime, and coaches went into another room to talk. One of the team captains would write on the board:

- What they did right in 1st half
- What they do wrong in 1st half
- What they needed to change for 2nd half

Then the coaches would come in and talk about 2nd half strategy.

When she was a young coach, she said there was a disconnect between her and the team.

She said she ASSUMED her players knew what she knew.

She said she ASSUMED when she coached; they were on the same page.

She felt she was "leading by assumption".

She realized the best way to know where the players were, was by using the chalkboard to see what her players were thinking.

She could see if they knew what they did right.

She could see if they knew what they did wrong.

In just a few seconds, she could tell if her players understood the context of the game.

Once she found out where they were, she would coach them from that point.

She said, as a leader, you must find out where your people are before you can lead them.

Leadership by assumption will always cause us to have a disconnect.

Coach Summit helped us see; you have to find out where your team is before leading them.

As the leader, you must always ask yourself what must I do and say to connect with my people? And finally, what questions should I be asking to find out where they are?

Below are five questions I like to ask my employees to help identify their strengths:

1. Where can you perform in your profession or personal life to distinction?
2. What skills and activities have accounted for your greatest successes to date?
3. What comes easy to you right now?
4. During which task do you lose track of time?
5. Why do you enjoy doing that specific task?

Consistency tells the story of your strengths. Boost your priorities by harnessing your concentration. Dwell on your strengths, not your weaknesses. John C. Maxwell writes about focus in his book 21 Indispensable Qualities of a Leader; In chapter 8, he discusses the 70/25/5 principle.

- Devote 70% of your time and resources to developing your current strengths,
- 25% to developing new strengths and
- 5% to improve any weaknesses.

Stick to your strengths and delegate to cover your weak areas. Considering your priorities, determine how to take your strengths to the next level.

Baseball great Tony Gwynn devotes a considerable percentage of his time and effort to reviewing baseball videotapes of his batting. His intense focus on his performance has made him the greatest hitter in the last 50 years. Gwynn has batted over 300 in every season; people like him have cultivated a kind of concentration unknown to most people.

Identify Development Needs

After identifying an employee's strengths, take time to identify their development needs. Again, ask the employee to list what they consider are areas in need of development. Draw on supervisor and peer evaluations, your evaluation of the employee, and other data (such as sales reports or other such data) to locate the areas of development opportunity. When discussing these areas with the employee, focus on the potential for development and improvement rather than blame or punishment. Rather than framing them as things the employee does "wrong" or "poorly," frame them as opportunities to build new strengths or learn new skills. When possible, map these development needs to the employee's areas of strength or to the competencies they wish to develop to move into management.

Follow up developmental feedback by identifying steps the employee can take to build these areas into strengths. Simply giving developmental feedback with no plan may leave the employee feeling helpless or hopeless. Instead, make the employee aware of available tools or resources to develop their development areas.

3 questions to ask to identify developmental needs:

1. What tasks do I consistently procrastinate doing?
2. I see anxiety when asked to do...?

3. The least fun part of my job responsibility is...?

Provide Development Opportunities

When you have discussed the employee's strengths and development needs, work with the employee to make a development plan. Provide opportunities to address development needs through mentoring, internal training, external training, or on-the-job practice. Have the employee set goals and benchmarks for their development and set up times to check-in or evaluate progress. Keep the focus positive rather than punitive.

Essentially, you are helping your employee put together a SWOT analysis of their career or career path.

We usually complete a SWOT analysis for different projects, programs, and marketing presentations. However, we need to start doing these more often for career development. If you do a web search, you will find a lot of free templates online to complete a SWOT analysis.

In addition, make the employee aware of any programs or tools that the organization has, such as peer mentoring groups or training workshops that might help them develop the identified areas. This process should also be ongoing – help the employee identify opportunities to focus on development and provide new opportunities regularly. I have found that some managers are not vested in their teams' growth and development. What I mean by that is some managers will say they are; however, if they are not willing to pay for the class or associated travel so the employee can attend, then they truly are NOT invested in the employee. If you are not willing to pay for it, what you are saying is, "I am not interested in helping my team grow." Leaders never say that; however, managers do. If you find yourself in that predicament, ask yourself, do you want that employee to be around ten years from now still thinking the same way? Or do you want to bring out the best in your team?

> *"The first step in helping another person's ability to achieve is to help them believe they can."*
> *—John C. Maxwell*

On The Life Sciences Trainers & Educators Network (LTEN) website, there is a quick self-assessment tool that helps you understand if you are an empowering leader who likes to help develop future leaders *(See Note #1 for information to access)*.

<u>Ways to evaluate if you are an empowering leader.</u>
(rate these 1-10: 1 = I Never 10 = I Always)

- Do I believe in people and believe they are the org most appreciable asset?
- Do I feel that team leadership can accomplish more than individual leadership?
- Do I look for potential leaders and quickly assimilate them into the org?
- Do I desire to raise others above my level of leadership?
- What happens when I bring someone into my department and realize they are quicker than I am?
- Do I invest time in developing people that have leadership potential?
- Where am I spending my time?
- Do I enjoy watching others get credit for what I have taught them?
- Are do I want to get the credit
- Do I allow the freedom of thought and the process, or do I have to be in control?

- Do I give my influence publicly to potential leaders as possible?
- Give credit to them in front of their spouse or significant other. That's important, and you gain respect.
- Do I have a succession plan to have others take my position?
- Do I hand the baton off to a teammate and truly root for them?

Empowering Leadership Spectrum Scorecard

If you scored 100 – Congratulations! You are an Empowering Leader!

If you scored 90 to 99, pat yourself on the back. You are well on your way to becoming an empowering leader.

If you scored 75 to 90, you have built the foundation of effective leadership. Examine areas where you need to strengthen.

If you scored 50 to 74, you are doing OK as a leader, but you have the potential to do much better.

If you scored below 50, you have a lot of work to do as a leader. The good news is that you can practice these skills at work, at home, and in the community.

You have the responsibility to empower, help build and grow potential leaders on your team. You should take that responsibility seriously and be willing to help someone else grow.

Practical Illustration

In his annual review, Patrick's supervisor Yvette asked if he had ever considered moving into a managerial position.

"Yes," Patrick replied, "but he didn't think he had the skills needed to be a good manager." Yvette offered to spend time with Patrick evaluating his skills with those common to good managers. She used a list created by their organization that listed ten core competencies of good managers, with examples of each.

After she and Patrick reviewed it, they spent 15 minutes discussing the areas in which Patrick felt his skills were strong and 15 additional minutes discussing areas in which he wanted to improve. Patrick realized that he had solid time management and interpersonal skills, which would serve him well as a manager. Patrick and Yvette agreed that he would need to build skills in managing people and budgets but that his strengths would also serve him well in these areas. Yvette gave Patrick information about an internal training offered by their Learning and Development department about effectively managing employees, and he signed up.

CHAPTER 4

TURNING YOUR ORDINARY INTO EXTRAORDINARY

> *"When you become a leader, get help. The temptation is to come across as omniscient and omnipotent: I know everything; I'm all-powerful. I don't need any help; help is a weakness. The person is in trouble. And that person will have no safety net when they fall."* — *John Bacon*

You are a leader; now what? Grab a beverage of your choice and whatever you prefer to capture your notes on, and travel with me down memory lane. Can you ever remember having a mentor in your life? Maybe your first mentor was a parent, relative, teacher, neighbor, or friend? Jot down any names that come to mind.

Do you remember what that person taught you? Do you recall how they taught you? Do you still perform the activities they led you through? Write down anything you can remember about your experiences with that person.

At this point, you are probably thinking, I had a coach that showed me these things, and I had a mentor that did the exact same thing. You may also be asking if there is a difference between a mentor and a coach? They seem very similar. According to Merriam-Webster dictionary, the essential meaning of mentor is someone who teaches or gives help and advice to a less experienced and often younger person. According to the Cambridge English Dictionary, a coach is someone whose job is to teach people to improve at a sport, skill, or school subject. For example, a tennis coach is someone whose job is to train and organize a sports team. By way of this chapter, I want to help simplify what mentoring is and how you can turn your ordinary into Extraordinary by becoming the best mentor you can be.

My early mentor was my mom. She loved to cook and was a good "southern" cook. She allowed me to start learning how to cook before pre-school. It began with simple items that evolved more into just preparing the meal. For example, my mom taught me how to set the table with the proper placement of the utensils and glassware. I also learned many science lessons from the cooking lessons. The measurements and ingredients helped me know that the item I was preparing wouldn't turn out well if I didn't include them. The lessons my mom taught me in the kitchen were invaluable to life.

For example, every cake doesn't always turn out the same. Even though it is the same recipe, the same ingredients, the same oven, the weather that day may be different, affecting the total outcome. Fast forward a few years, my mom stepped off a street curb and fell to her knees while holding my baby brother in her arms. Fortunately, my baby brother was only a little shaken up. My mom was okay except for some bummed-up knees where she would need complete bed rest and stay completely off them for several weeks. She was laid up in bed while I had to step up and take care of the rest of the family. I was thankful for the many years that my mom mentored me. I was able to take on more responsibilities in the family to help out during the crucial time when my mom and my baby brother needed me the most. Because of how my mom had mentored me years before, I never once in any way questioned my confidence. I knew what I needed to know; I stepped up, took charge, and never looked back. When I stepped up, I never doubted my self-confidence when the time arose. I had learned the actual value of mentoring at a young age.

If you ask an excellent manager where they learned how to manage, the answer will likely be from a manager who was essential to their career and impacted them the most. It could be something they learned early on that has stuck with them through many years and has formed the way they lead. While courses and training on management skills are valuable and have their place, people often learn the most about managing by *being managed*. You probably think that a "bad" manager can provide valuable lessons in what not to do; people know more about management by being managed well. From my experience, employees who work more effectively tend to be happier and have more productive environments.

Are You Waiting? Pair New Managers with Mentors

Mentoring is invaluable when developing new managers, whether they are freshly in the position or on the management track for the future. I remember hearing these words when I first transitioned into a new management role. "You are in charge of your development."

Well, I thought I knew what that meant, but I wasn't sure what I didn't know. In my mind, I felt that people would have a vested interest in me to help set me up for success.

Instead of asking great questions, I tried to crack the secret code, which was the biggest mistake in my leadership career. Have you ever tried to crack the code to break into the inner circle? You know the inner circle that seems everyone knows the code to gain entry but you? Every person has been "new" at something at one time or another. Have you ever felt like you were thrown into the fire, and you were all alone with no help from a friend? Don't sit back and wait for "them" to come to you; get up and become the fire! Go after it!

It took time to build rapport and relationships on the corporate level, to figure out "if" they wanted to help me and how they wanted to help me. Soon, I began to make connections, and along came my corporate mentor friend. I learned that not everybody wanted to stick their neck out to help me. It was vital for me to select my mentor because I believed my core values needed to align with theirs.

Mentoring relationships give employees a chance to see good management "in action" and seek feedback from someone they respect. Mentors can help provide development opportunities and serve as valuable sounding boards for new managers. For example, my corporate mentor nominated me to lead a statewide project which included emceeing the all-day event. The exposure developed on a foundation of trust where my mentor gave me a chance to shine beyond my wildest dreams. Indeed, it was about being my authentic self, building relationships, and watching the doors begin to open for me. I was living my dream, and you can live yours too!

The foundation stones for a balanced success are honesty,
character, integrity, faith, love, and loyalty.
— Zig Ziglar

What Motivates You to Become an Effective Manager? As a mentor, what will you offer to someone one day?

My corporate mentor taught me about Servant Leadership. A leadership philosophy in which an individual interacts with others - either in a management or fellow employee capacity - to achieve authority rather than power. The authority figure intends to promote the well-being of those around them. One of the surest ways to encourage and reinforce quality management is to reward effective managers. When employees see effective managers being recognized and rewarded, they aspire to demonstrate the same traits as these individuals.

Depending on your company culture, rewards for effective managers may be financial (pay raises or bonuses), incentives (extra vacation time), symbolic (plaques or certificates), or a mix of the three. Finding out what motivates individual managers and tailoring the rewards is also an effective strategy. Whatever reward system you choose, take the time not only to reward effective managers but recognize their efforts in a public way. Recognition among the company will go a long way to bring a team together and bring out the best in your leaders.

Emulate Effective Managers

Let's go back to the list you started at the beginning of this chapter. Maybe you will have new people rise to the top of the list as you focus on these questions:

1. Who was the best manager you ever had? What qualities did they demonstrate?
2. As a new or aspiring manager, in what ways can you emulate your best manager?
3. How can you encourage employees to seek out effective managers and identify positive traits they can emulate?

Believe it or not, you have had opportunities woven throughout your life to become a part of who you are. So, stop telling yourself you've never been a leader or a mentor. You have real-life experiences in your toolbox, and some of those tools just need to be polished. You have more things going for you than you realize.

New Leader Action Plan Next Steps

It is important to let a new manager/leader own their development. They need to have awareness for understanding what they need to know. They need to see the audience they are speaking with and what they are trying to accomplish.

1. There are many ways to be an effective manager. Each organization's culture will influence the type of management it values. Creating and documenting a set of best management practices helps to reinforce the organizational culture. It serves as a resource for new and experienced managers.

    *   A best practices document need not be extensive or exhaustive. It should be a living document that can change as new practices emerge. Working with employees at multiple levels, identify what management practices and behaviors are identified consistently as effective, engaging, and motivating. I highly suggest this is visible where others can add to the document, and the team grows faster together.

2. Review organizational policies (such as hiring and termination) and develop a set of best practices based on these. Adopting a central location of best practices help ensure consistency and serves as another guidepost for managers to develop and grow.

- If you could pick one person to mentor you, who would it be and why?
- What would be the topic used that you could mentor someone?

Role clarity in a mentor relationship

Do you trust your mentor relationship?

- What are the qualities you see in a good mentor?
- Why is it essential in leadership for mentors to be successful?
- How do you find a good mentor?
- What happens if your mentor doesn't walk the talk?

I wrote this with you in mind, whether you are a brand-new leader who needs additional growth or an experienced leader who needs to find their purpose and reinvent yourself. There is always someone that could use your expertise. Mentoring is about developing future generations, and there is always room for you to turn your ordinary into EXTRAordinary.

"A man must be big enough to admit his mistakes, smart enough to profit from them, and strong enough to correct them."—John C. Maxwell

Practical Illustration

Tina was recently connected with her leadership mentor, Tom, as part of her new manager development plan. Tina had a great deal of respect for Tom and admired how he managed his employees and dealt with the poor work morale in his department.

Tina asked Tom how he remained so positive and calm with the chaos happening in his department?

"I had a great boss and mentor in my first supervisory role," Todd told her. "Carla was always looking for the positive. She was a half-full cup type of person. Carla told me once that focusing on the negative drains your energy and creates additional stress amongst your team, but people pull together when you focus on the positive or the common goal. So, I try to keep the focus on the goal, not the stress or the problems."

The more time Tina spent with Todd, the more she learned. Finally, Tina decided to adopt Todd's attitude of focusing on the positive with her direct reports.

CHAPTER 5

PROVIDE EFFECTIVE TOOLS

A key component to developing new managers is providing them with the tools needed to succeed. Just as you wouldn't expect an employee to do a job without supplies or necessary technology, you cannot expect managers to manage effectively without a tool kit. Take the time to create or locate the tools managers need to lead effectively and develop their skills and competencies. These might include technology, documents and policies, opportunities, and relationships. When new managers are well equipped to execute their duties and continuously develop, everyone benefits.

Providing practical tools is so critical to helping new managers start strong. It is so essential that without it, they typically will fail early and often. I like to put things in mathematical formulas to help illustrate my point.

Quality Leadership (QL) = P3 * Empowerment (E)

P3 = **Provide** Manuals/Policy Documents + **Provide** Support + **Provide** Development Opportunities

If no P3 * **E, then** no QL

P3 * E = QL

So, in other words, Quality Leadership happens when new managers are empowered and provided with manuals & policy documents, support, and development opportunities. As it stands, quality leadership usually cannot happen without those things.

Provide Manuals and Policy Documents

Manuals and policy documents are invaluable to a new manager. These documents are an essential roadmap to the day-to-day aspects of the job. Policy documents should be provided as early as possible, especially for those policies that the manager must enforce or follow. This allows the new manager time to review the guidelines and ask questions about implementing or following them. Copies of these documents should be readily available, either in digital or hardcopy form. Policies must be regularly updated as processes change as well. Manuals are also vital; as they provide a sense of structure to the job duties, the organizational culture, and the manager's expectations. A quality manual allows a manager to problem-solve and answer questions in many cases, saving time and empowering. Manuals should also be living documents, regularly updated.

Empower New Managers

Empowering new managers is key to their development and success. If a new manager feels that they must have every decision or action signed off on or approved by someone higher up, this stunts that manager's growth and development. Make clear to new managers that you and other experienced managers are resources, but they can and should make decisions and take actions independently. A clear set of job responsibilities (in the manual) helps here, as new managers have a sense of what decisions and actions are theirs to take and which require input from others. Encourage new managers and those in development to be managers by voicing opinions or offering ideas. Empower new managers by allowing them to make mistakes or fix problems rather than stepping in yourself.

Empowering leaders give their power away intentionally. Empowered Leaders are secure in their skills, abilities and they understand the value they bring. I once worked for a leader who was empowering others. He always made time if we needed it but never gave us the answer. He would ask excellent questions to help go within to find the answer. Then he would follow up to ensure we were okay with the next action steps. In turn, he never had to worry about his leadership team delivering on expectations.

> Law of Empowerment states, "Only secure leaders give power to others." — John C. Maxwell

This law illustrates the phrase, "it is far better to give than receive," that giving will be returned to you exponentially.

President Abraham Lincoln, recognizing his weaknesses, intentionally empowered those around him to make him and his administration stronger.

The Lesson: Empowering those around you or on your team will build their strength and allow them to maximize the contribution of their skill set.

Provide Support

Even as you seek to empower new managers, provide support. Those new to management may be hesitant to take action or nervous about exerting authority. Let new managers, and those in development to be new managers, know that there is support for them.

Here are two statements you should say more often to uplevel your leadership with new managers.

- **I have confidence in your ability to lead this project.**
  - When you display confidence in someone, they will work hard to meet your belief in them.
  - On the other hand, they will also meet that belief system when you don't believe in them.
  - Sometimes people need to borrow your confidence in them to succeed, so lend it.

- **What can I do to help you be successful?**
  - Just offering to help, you earn respect.
  - Your team member will be amazingly pleased to know you have their back.

Try this every day this week and watch how your team or teammates start to thrive.

One of the most straightforward steps you can take is not second-guessing or undermining a new manager with their direct reports. If you have questions about an action or decision, address them privately with the new manager. Also, encourage new managers to continue to work with their mentors so that they have support as they transition to the new role. Making new managers aware of other support systems, such as peer networks, discussion groups, reading materials, and resource people, is another critical way to support them as they grow and develop.

To provide support to a new manager, you must have a high Emotional Intelligence (EQ); you must already be operating at the next level. Unfortunately, most leaders don't know who they are, so they struggle to help other leaders, especially their own team.

Jeremie Kubicek and Steve Cockram authored *"100X Leader: How to Become Someone Worth Following."* I believe it should be a must-read of all leaders, so I recommend you do if you have not read it. In the book, they write, "You can't become a 100X leader if you're stuck operating at 80% or 90%". They provide the following assessment tool to help you become a better leader. 100X Leader: How to Become Someone Worth Following is a good tool for new managers.

> *"The Sherpa don't celebrate how many times they personally have been to the summit, but how many times they help others get to the top."* — *100X Leader*

Please take this short assessment but be honest with yourself; it is not punitive; it is a tool that can help you and your leaders to become better leaders.

On a 1 to 10 scale – where ten is the best – take this "100% health check" to see where you stand as a leader:

- You are confident about your leadership abilities.
- You lead a healthy and rewarding life that keeps you "present and productive."
- You have a healthy emotional IQ to lead people even in complex circumstances.
- You do your best to make rational – not emotional – decisions.
- You understand and accept your leadership responsibilities. You know where you're going and are determined to lead others at the highest level.
- As a leader, you feel "physically, mentally, and emotionally" fit.

After rating yourself against these standards, total your overall score and divide by six.

- If it's seven or better, great! You're a healthy leader.
- If it's five or less, you have work to do. To become a better leader, work on mastering yourself first.

Where do you fall on the scale?

1_____2_____3_____4_____5_____6_____7
_____8_____9_____10

Provide Training and Development Opportunities

Every new manager will need some training and development as they step into a new role, and every employee needs ongoing training and development to reach their full potential. As you create a path to management and identify critical skills and competencies, provide training and development opportunities that will allow new managers, and those on a path to leadership, to grow.

You might develop internal training, such as workshops geared towards managers and those who aspire to management. Bringing in outside trainers, or making employees aware of outside seminars and activities, is another way to offer diverse experiences. If possible, the organization should pay for or otherwise subsidize external training. Less formal opportunities, such as inviting an employee on the management path to sit in on meetings or help design documentation for a department, are also meaningful. Work with Human Resources/Learning and Development and other divisions to create, offer, or make employees aware of different skill-building opportunities.

As mentioned in Chapter 3, I required all employees to take one development training class each year. It was a fundamental step to ensuring my team continued to grow. It was also essential to help my team understand that I valued them and wanted to help them be more valuable to the organization. It is worth repeating here, don't be a leader who is bogged down with what will this cost my department for you to take this training course. It would help if you were looking at this as an investment in the future of the team, department, and company. Investing in training is as critical as investing in the R&D pipeline.

Organizations that don't properly invest in training for their people will soon find themselves out of business, falling behind their competition, and losing top talent to growth-oriented organizations.

Look at yourself and your organization and decide if you have 1s and 2s coming in the door and staying or 8s and 9s leaving. You may be doing something wrong if you do. Look at your professional growth and development plan. People quit if they are not growing. Let me repeat that, people leave if they are not growing.

Peter Drucker had it right when he said leadership does the right things.

> "Management is doing things right; leadership is doing the right things." — Peter Drucker

In the book 100 Ways to Motivate Others, the author tells us, "The greatest source of stress in the workplace is the mind's attempt to carry many thoughts, many tasks, many future scenarios, many cares, many worries, many concerns at once. The mind can't do that. No mind can; Not even Einstein's could".

When managers develop into leaders, they realize it is essential to focus on one thing at a time. Too many managers don't know this yet, and that is why they are managers and not leaders.

Great leaders understand this subtle difference.

The only difference between ordinary leaders and EXTRAordinary leaders is EXTRA.

The only difference between winning and losing in leadership is belief.

The only difference between hot water and boiling water is 1 degree.

At 211°, water is hot

At 212°, it boils

And with boiling water; comes steam.

And that steam can power a locomotive.

The EXTRA degree makes all the difference.

The only difference between a manager reaching their full potential and not reaching their full potential is desire.

If you intentionally add value to your team daily, you will receive exponential growth out of your team. It doesn't take much to help your team go from ordinary to EXTRAordinary. You must be willing to use the formula mentioned earlier in this chapter: **P3 * E = QL.** It is not that difficult.

Practical Illustration

Working with his supervisor, Craig started on the management track at his company. While his supervisor, Laura, was very supportive, he sometimes felt unsure about the next step in his career. He was very nervous about stepping fully into a management role, especially personnel decisions and policy. Although he was very skilled at the technical aspects of his job, Craig was less comfortable managing people and making hiring decisions.

Laura often told him not to worry about it; she would take care of the issue.

In talking to a colleague, Wayne, a manager for several years, Craig learned that the company had a comprehensive manual to personnel policies. There was also a workshop, offered every six weeks, on interpersonal skills for managers. Craig got a copy of the manual and signed up for the workshop. He soon felt much more comfortable with this aspect of his job.

CHAPTER 6

FIND THE NEED THEN LEAD

The challenging work of developing and supporting a new manager begins with the promotion. It continues as they transition to their new role. While many senior leaders focus on investing in training, assigning a mentor, random check-ins, they fail to consider new managers' personal, mental, and relational needs. During times of crisis like the pandemic, I personally learned that new managers face emotional challenges and the need to develop the skills to be successful.

Like a photograph, life isn't made in the bright moments. We develop from all the negatives. It takes darkness and challenges to reveal the beauty underneath.

In the spring of 2021, I went through a depression due to personal issues I was trying to work through alone. Although friends and loved ones surrounded me, I did not share how sad I was with anyone.

As a person of faith, I turned to prayer. I could not explain the craziness that had me stuck, but I did find some relief.

However, I knew something was missing.

During the pandemic, I launched a new Leadership coaching business. I also run a youth nonprofit organization with volunteer staff, and I have a full-time job. I tried to shake the feelings off to be a strong leader while hiding behind the pain, shame, and guilt. I was dying on the inside because I wasn't getting enough of what I needed to grow and thrive. I could not understand why I kept going deeper into the dark.

I attempted to remain connected to the groups I was affiliated with, especially the John Maxwell leadership team and Toastmasters.

Finally, after several months of struggling in the dark, I decided to talk to my best friend. It was not until then that I began to see some light. I decided to seek out a therapist. That is when the weights finally started to fall off because I had an opportunity to be true to myself. The therapist asked hard questions and told me that it didn't make sense to seek help if I couldn't own my truth. That's when the healing began. I learned that you heal if you're unwilling to reveal, which is why I want to approach this chapter from a different leadership angle. Darkness is an absence of a "thing," and we often stay away from the light because we don't want to face that "thing," whatever it may be.

Ask for help

Many leaders don't ask for fear of appearing incompetent or weak. When I started asking for help, it changed the trajectory of my life as an individual and as a leader. As leaders, we tend to hide our humanity, forgetting that our fears and doubts are normal.

When developing new managers, build support systems that address managers' personal, mental, and relational needs. When support systems are in place and those systems are readily accessible, employees are much more likely to access them. Having the support of peers and mentors is key to a new manager's success. In turn, today's new managers will become tomorrow's support system for the next generation of managers.

Managers know there is no punishment for asking for help.

Support Systems

When we experience new things, we also drain ourselves. Overworking leaves us feeling like dead batteries. Likewise, daily things like work drain our energy, and it's important to remember to recharge.

Leaders do many things right, like running companies well, but may have a relational deficit. This happens when they don't have enough of the right kind of people to keep life fulfilled.

In *People Fuel: Fill Your Tank for Life, Love, and Leadership*, author John Townsend teaches that "finding a social support and growth system is very important and advises business leaders to create a life team to engage in growth; on a structured level."

He offers the following criteria:

- Intentionally select a set of people who will become your primary source for relational nutrients.
  - The main focus is growth – transferring relational nutrients to one another, resulting in better personal, relational, spiritual, and emotional life.
  - Leaders need a space to fill up their gas tanks. They need a mutual transfer of nutrients, not a delivery of nutrients from the leader to the group.
- A Life Team member needs to be committed to self-improvement and doing something about it. Their calendar should reflect some commitment to continuously becoming a better person. They may have a coach, mentor, spiritual director, counselor, or small

group. But they are putting energy into some source of information and experience that leads to change.

- Life Team members need to be oriented to seek each other's best, no matter what. There must be no condemnation or judgment of one another.
  - When you care for someone, your highest value is that you provide good for them, in whatever form they need. You can disagree and have differences. But ultimately, Life Team members need to know and experience that they are on each other's side and have their backs.

Encourage Peer Networking

Peer networks are a powerful form of support for new managers. When interacting with peers who are either at the same stage of their careers or who have recently had similar experiences, new managers may feel more comfortable asking questions or expressing fears or concerns than they might be with superiors. Cohorts of peers who enter management at about the same time can also serve as support during the transition and learning process. Encourage peer networking at your organization. Some organizations create formal peer support groups, where employees at a similar career stage meet regularly to support each other. Informal networking is also valuable. Encourage new managers to reach out to their peers in other departments or the same department in different locations of your organization. Also, encourage established managers to reach out to new managers. Foster an environment where peers support and collaborate.

Establish Resource People

Establish a network of "go-to" people and make new managers aware of this network. Including a list or table in the manual given to new managers is an effective strategy. New managers might find it helpful, for example, to have a resource person in Human Resources to answer personnel questions, a resource person for questions about budgets, or a resource person who handles ordering supplies. When a new manager has a network of expert resources at their fingertips, this empowers action and decision making. It also fosters efficiency, as the manager can go directly to someone who can answer a question or solve a problem.

Julie Zhuo, the author of *The Making of a Manager,* says, "to manage people well, you must develop trusting relationships with them, understand their strengths and weaknesses (as well as your own), make good decisions about who should do what (including hiring and firing when necessary), and coach individuals to do their best".

Effective leadership learns to broker the gifts and talents on their team and place individuals in the appropriate tasks according to their gifts. You should know the keys to their heart – what do they dream about, cry about, and why are they singing?

Establish regular Check-ins

Transitioning to any new role is an adjustment, whether you're coming up within an organization or coming in from outside. However, new managers are likely to have questions or anxieties, especially early on. Establish regular check-in times to set aside time to check progress, answer questions, or provide feedback. Ensure that the new manager knows that these check-ins are not about micromanaging or punishment but rather an investment in their development. You might check in once a week for the first few months that a new manager is in their role, then transition to once every two weeks or once a month after some time has passed. Work with the employee to find what works best for both of you. You may do check-ins face to face, over the phone, or email, depending on what you and the new manager prefer and need.

Conclusion:

I have personally learned that relational nutrients are essential to growth and physical nutrients to our bodies. When we don't intake the right amounts of nutrients over the right amount of time, we risk damage: personal, relational, and work problems. However, when we are full of the right sorts of nutrients, we think clearly, feel the energy, and make good decisions.

Three tips for developing managers:

1. Make sure new managers aren't thrust into their new role without a transitional period
    *   Example: Create a 90-Day Plan for new Managers (include the development of people skills)
2. Beware of the "comfort zone" trap of overmanaging the functions you know well and undermanaging the people.
3. Determine what managers need from you
    *   Do a needs analysis to determine the strengths and areas that need improvement.

Practical Illustration:

One summer, a new intern took down a major social media platform by accidentally introducing a bad error into the codebase. As everyone worked madly to fix the mistake, the manager caught a glimpse of his pale face. The manager was sure he thought he was going to be fired.

He wasn't. His manager apologized instead for not setting him up with the right tools to succeed in his role. Other engineers took accountability for not catching the error beforehand. The entire team then participated in a post-incident debrief to understand why the failure happened and how to prevent similar issues in the future.

CHAPTER 7

IDENTIFY STRONG CANDIDATES EARLY

While every organization is likely to do a mix of internal promotions and outside hiring, the best candidates for management are often within your organization. Suppose you wait to develop potential new managers until you have to fill a vacant position; you may miss out on some talented employees. Identifying strong candidates for management roles should be an ongoing process. Employees with management aspirations and potential should be recognized as early as possible. This allows the organization and the employee to invest time and resources in developing that potential.

Every winning team understands the value of having great depth. They know the starters will carry the heavy load; however, they expect the bench players to relieve when needed. The Pittsburgh Steelers won 4 Superbowl rings in the 1970s with starters like Terry Bradshaw, Mean Joe Greene, Lynn Swan, Franco Harris, Donnie Shell, you heard all the names. However, they still had great depth in each area, just if one of the starters got hurt.

Here are a few names of talented backups on the Pittsburgh Steelers team you may not know:

Andy Russell: 7x Pro Bowl, 4x All-Pro, 2x Super Bowl Champion Linebacker

JT Thomas: One Pro Bowl 4X Super Bowl Champion Corner

Mike Wagner: **2x Pro Bowl, 2x All-Pro, 4x Super Bowl Champion Safety**

Larry Brown: **3x Pro Bowl, 4x Super Bowl Champion Tight-End**

Benny Cunningham: **2x Super Bowl Champion Tight-End**

Roy Gerela: **2x Pro Bowl, 3x Super Bowl Champion, 1x PFW Golden Toe Award Kicker**

Ronnie Shanklin: **1x Pro Bowl, 1x Super Bowl Champion Wide Receiver**

Glen Edwards: **2x Pro Bowl, 3x All-Pro, 2x Super Bowl Champion Safety**

> *"The secret is to work less as individuals and more as a team. As a coach, I play not my eleven best, but my best eleven." — Knute Rockne*

This same approach and philosophy need to be pervasive in your organization when it pertains to building talent from within.

Development Begins Early

Employee development at all levels should be ongoing, of course. When it comes to new managers, development must begin early. Waiting until there is a vacant position to develop an employee with potential means trying to rush the process, which is stressful for all involved. Instead, begin developing employees who show interest and potential for management at the earliest opportunity.

In some ways, this can be a company-wide initiative, with training and workshops. Individual development with employees who desire to move into management should also begin as soon as possible. In this way, the organization has many talented potential managers in the pipeline when positions need to be filled.

A Harvard Business Review study titled "*Why We Wait So Long to Train Our Leaders*" by Jack Zenger shows that the average age of employees in leadership development programs is 42 – much older than the average age of an employee in a leadership role, which is 30. The study reveals that employees occupy leadership roles for approximately a decade before undergoing any training.

If you wouldn't take math lessons from someone who isn't a math pro, then why would you trust an untrained leader to run your team?

Why do some organizations wait too long to train potential leaders?

I believe the #1 reason is a lack of trust. Employees do not trust leadership, and leadership does not have confidence in lower-level employees. When there is a lack of trust in any culture, dysfunction happens, and this dysfunction leads to no training, disengagement, low morale, and less than stellar performance.

In 2019, Shelley D. Smith, best-selling author, consultant, and Founder & CEO of Premier Rapport consulting firm wrote, "A lack of trust in the workplace is the virus that can create a diseased workplace culture. It often begins with leadership and spreads throughout the team, leading to a cycle of unhealthy responses that affect engagement and productivity. Team members who don't trust their leaders are likely working the bare minimum and planning to get out. They're probably not innovating because they don't believe what you tell them. A smart team member will bide their time until they leave. This isn't what you want as a leader, as it doesn't create an environment that allows an organization to thrive. If you don't trust your team, you're likely either micromanaging or withholding information and working on initiatives on your own or with a select group of people. This can create a vicious cycle, as your team may respond by pulling back even further, so you've created a perfect storm in this self-fulfilling prophecy of distrust."

As a leader, you should be asking yourself the following questions to help you continually build your bench. I recommend you think about these questions twice per year.

- Whom should I be developing now?
- Why would I not develop this person now?
- What development do they need now?
- How can I best develop this person now?

Notice that these questions all end with the word **now**. It is imperative that you consider the current environment and the long-term needs. **Now** is all about the person who needs to be trained.

However, it would help evaluate the organization's long-term needs (next year, five years from now). What training can you do **now** that will help them and the organization in the future?

Identify Candidates Early

Not every employee will have management aspirations, and not every employee who aspires to management will succeed. However, it is vital to alert employees who want to eventually enter management, who show strong potential for leadership, or who otherwise appear to be "management material." Identifying these employees early in their time at your organization gives you the greatest opportunity to help them grow and develop.

I remember being promoted to a Product Manager in our Global Marketing organization. On my first day in the office, my director asked two questions.

- What do I want to do next?
- How long would it take for me to put together a succession plan?

My initial thoughts were, what are you talking about? This is my first day.

He said, "I know. However, we need to plan today for what tomorrow will look like." He went on to say that if we don't do this today, we will always put it off for another day which will never come.

At that moment, my opinion about planning changed. I learned that planning today for tomorrow is a must.

We then created a succession plan and discussed what I wanted to do next. It allowed me to discuss my goals and gave my director ideas on how to help me in my current new role. It gave him an idea of what opportunities he should send my way, what connections he could help me with, and my development needs.

There are several ways to identify strong candidates for management. Employee evaluations or reviews are an excellent source, as you have the opportunity to examine the employee's skill set and discuss their goals. If an employee expresses management goals, you should explore this further. Highly productive or otherwise high-performing employees may also be candidates for management. Asking managers and supervisors to identify potential candidates among their direct reports is a third way to locate likely future managers. In all cases, please discuss their goals, what the management track involves, and whether they wish to move forward with the employee.

Identify Candidates Through Reviews

The employee performance review is perhaps the wealthiest source when seeking to identify strong candidates for management. Because the employee review offers a picture of the employee's strengths, development areas, and overall progress, you can quickly evaluate whether they possess some or all of the skills needed for management. The review also offers a chance to discuss their future employment goals with an employee, including whether they are interested in moving into management.

The professional development plan portion of the employee review, in which you work with them to set forth professional goals for the next year, is an excellent opportunity to discuss the management track and begin the development of an employee who expresses interest in management. Suppose your review process also includes evaluations from peers and colleagues. In that case, this information may also help you identify those employees who have the potential to be successful managers within your organization.

Be careful not to make this an annual process, however. In the past, some employee performance reviews were just a yearly exercise that did not make an impact. After the employee signed the performance document, no one would follow up on the things discussed during the review unless you were intentional about it.

In a 2016 Gallup survey on How Millennials Want to Work and Live, it stated:

- Millennials want to be free of old workplace policies and performance management standards. They expect leaders and managers to adapt accordingly.
- Millennials are the largest generational cohort in American history, with approximately ninety million members. Of these, roughly 43 percent are people of color. Millennials are a largely optimistic group, and they believe that life and work should be worthwhile and have meaning.
- Millennials are the least engaged people in the workplace.
  - 71% of millennials are not engaged (checked out) at work. (That's a miss on the employers' part)
  - Gallup estimates that millennial turnover due to lack of engagement costs the U.S. economy $30.5 BILLION ANNUALLY.
  - They want to feel connected to their work, not just "get by." They want to contribute.
- They change jobs more than other generations.
  - Companies are not giving them compelling reasons to stay. It's not just about collecting a paycheck.
    - 60% OF MILLENNIALS say they are open to a different job opportunity.
- Millennials are not pursuing job satisfaction; they are pursuing personal development.
  - They want to develop and grow to become a better person.
  - They want to do something of value and substance.
  - They are not just looking for bells and whistles, ping pong tables, fancy latte machines & free food.
  - Giving out toys and entitlements is a leadership mistake, and worse, it's condescending.

  ○ As consumers, millennials look for fun and entertaining experiences. But not as employees.

  ○ Purpose and development drive this generation.

Law of <u>Intentionality</u> - Growth doesn't just happen. You must be intentional about your growth.
—John C. Maxwell

Employers and their leaders can learn a lot from that Gallup survey on hiring and retaining millennials in the workplace. Again, this goes back to questions leaders and organizations should be asking during this process. Here are a few of the questions the leader should ask themself:

1. Am I providing the right opportunity to the right person?
2. Have I considered the employee's interest?
3. Does this person have the skill and will for this opportunity? If yes, what specific skill?
4. How does this match up with the organization's long-term needs?

The answers to these questions will help you select the right person for the right opportunity. It will also help determine if you keep the employee's interest in mind. Both parties have to be interested simultaneously to be effective and successful,

- If I'm selected, but I'm not interested = Unengaged Employee
- If I'm not selected, but I'm interested = Unhappy Employee
- If I'm selected, and I'm interested = Engaged and Creative employee

Develop Those with Management Goals

When an employee expresses having management goals, this is an opportunity to begin the development process. Not every employee with management goals will ultimately become a manager. However, investing in many potential candidates early on gives your organization the best chance of having a deep pool of talented candidates when management positions need to be filled. When an employee expresses a desire to transition into management, spend some time exploring this with them, discuss the management track, the critical milestones, and where the employee's career fits in relation to these. Identify strengths and development areas, and work with the employee to create a plan. Check-in with the employee regularly about this plan, even if it is just quarterly at review time. Identifying a group of potential candidates may be helpful. It allows you to create a peer cohort who can go through training and development experiences together and serve as support for one another. Do not discount an employee who expresses management goals, although you should honestly approach development needs.

As you work with your employee to develop goals, we need to make sure they are SMART goals. In case you have not heard about SMART goals, here is a brief overview:

SMART means Specific, Measurable, Attainable, Realistic, and Time-sensitive.

Specific: Don't be vague. Precisely what do you want?

Measurable: Quantify your goal. How will you know if you've achieved it or not?

Attainable: Be honest with yourself about what you can reasonably accomplish at this point in your life while considering your current responsibilities.

Realistic: It's got to be doable, honest, and practical.

Time: Associate a time frame with each goal. When should you complete the plan?

Practical Illustration

LaJuan didn't understand it. It seemed like every time he needed to fill a management position in his organization; he had an internal candidate who was almost perfect for the job but was lacking one or two key competencies or experiences. As a result, he ended up doing a lot of outside hiring, which often left his employees resentful at the lack of opportunity for advancement. He asked his colleague, Tammie, how she handled this issue in her division. Tammie replied that she was almost always able to hire internally.

LaJuan said, "You must have more motivated employees than I do."

"No," Tammie replied, "I start early. As soon as an employee expresses an interest in eventually becoming a manager, I help them make a plan for building the needed skills. When I hear of an employee that might be management material, I talk to them and see what potential is there. This way, I've always got people who are developing and ready to take on new roles."

CHAPTER 8

CLEARLY DEFINE
THE MANAGEMENT TRACK

The Power of a Clearly Defined Track

> *"No matter where you are in your life right now, and no matter where you have been, you are not yet all you can be"* — *Carly Fiorina*

Hola! My name is Johanna Rincón, and I am a leader like you. I consider myself a leader because I have developed the ability to influence others.

I want you to think about this for a moment; we are all leaders. Why? Because If you can influence someone else, then; that makes you are a leader.

The number one Leadership expert Dr. John C. Maxwell, says, "Leadership is all about influence, nothing more, nothing less."

When I started my career in the hospitality industry eighteen years ago as a front desk agent, I thought to myself, how can I get to the next level? How can I find out what I want?

Does any of these questions sound familiar? Have you asked yourself these questions too? I'm sure you have.

Even though I was not ready at that moment, I knew I needed to have clarity about where I wanted to go. Most importantly, I needed to have a plan of action to make it happen.

If you are currently an emerging manager/leader, you are about to get some great nuggets.

This chapter will share clear steps to transition from front-line staff to management.

Whether you're an individual who wants to take control of your professional development or a manager looking for ways to give your teams a clear and defined path to reach a management position, I recommend using this practical guide to design that explicit path.

Strategies covered in this chapter include:

- Learn to make your management track clear
- Discover why a clear path is a guidepost
- Understand why a clear way ensures quality training and support
- How to prepare for succession planning and management change
- Practical application to help you take action

Did you know that human potential is the only limitless resource in the world?

As you read this chapter, I hope you create a plan to live your full potential because that will allow you to promote beyond yourself. Most of us live our careers on autopilot (I know I did for a long time) without stopping for a moment and getting clear on what I wanted.

It can be challenging to decide confidently on your next career move and know if it will lead to more satisfaction, fulfillment, and success. Getting clarity on your desired career goal and development plan is your responsibility. It takes a lot of courage to fully acknowledge that you are the owner of the development, growth, and career journey you want to take.

By taking ownership, you will need to make consistent decisions and set clear career goals that are your own.

Here are a few reflection questions to make a clear and intentional career decision:

- What are my strengths?
- What are my values? What matters most to me?
- What do I want from my work-life and career?

As you reflect on these questions, think about this quote by *Marie Forleo, "Clarity comes from engagement, not through."*

Making the Track to Management Clear

"When you have clarity of intention, the universe
conspires with you to make it happen"
—Fabienne Fredrickson

When creating a management track for yourself or your team, clarity should always be the primary concern. Individuals who don't plan to move from their current positions into a managerial role are likely to become frustrated, feel there is no opportunity for advancement, and ultimately leave for other opportunities. I remember that's what happened to someone I met many years ago in New York. I will call this person Liz. She was a supervisor in a hotel and was hungry to learn and advance in her career. While she thought she had clarity on where she wanted to be, it became evident that three essential things were missing:

- Clear expectations
- Clear requirements
- Clear benchmark

Liz decided to pursue another opportunity. During the interview process with a new organization, she discovered a sense of clear direction, structure, and support to grow and develop her career. Liz was offered the job with the new organization, and it was what she needed. Before moving forward, she asked herself some key questions before making this critical decision in her career.

Questions You Should Ask Yourself Before Accepting a Job Offer

- Does my why align with the company's why and culture?
- Will this role challenge me? Will I advance my career working here?
- Is this job the next step in achieving my ultimate career goal?
- Does the company offer the benefits and salary I'm looking to have?
- Am I excited about the job/company?

The organization should clearly understand the process of keeping talent within an organization and ensuring that talented employees can advance. Creating a management track that provides clear expectations, requirements, and benchmarks will help individuals stay focused on their short-term and long-term goals. And no two employees will follow precisely the same career trajectory. Still, a clear general path from lower-level positions into management can apply to most situations.

This clear path will give you a sense of the education and training you need to move into management. For instance, intermediate positions you assume between your current and future management roles must be explicit. A flow chart or graphic may also be helpful for you in this process. Most importantly, the path should be easy to follow and understand, with clear connections between each step.

A Clear Path Is a Guidepost

"Leadership is the capacity to translate vision into reality" — Warren Bennis

One of the essential roles a clear management track serves is to be a guidepost. When you are ready to advance to the next level and have a laid-out management track, you can use it to shape your development efforts and professional goals. Whether you need to build skills, intermediate positions, or education you must attain, a clear management track can provide the backbone for an effective development plan.

Before diving into your professional development plan, let me ask you a question.

Do you have a Personal Development Plan?

I know for many years I didn't have one. I was doing what I knew was the right thing to do to hopefully someday get somewhere in life. I know I was getting things done, and good things were happening to me, but there was no real plan or intentionality behind my daily actions. It was not until I came across the law of intentionality that I discovered, "Growth Doesn't Just Happen: not for me, not for you, not for anybody." You have to go after it.

Now that I understand the importance of my personal development, I am intentional. I take personal responsibility in identifying where I am, where I want to be, and how I will get there. That is why I want to help you get clarity from this chapter. Having a development plan enables you to gain clarity, recognize where you have learning and development gaps, and allows you to identify resources to bridge those gaps. Did you know that growth's highest reward is not what we get from it but what we become because of it? Let me share with you some principles I practice in my career that will help you be intentional with your development plan:

Focus on priorities

- Implement what you are learning
- Reflect on what happens
- Seek feedback and support
- Transfer what you are learning to others

As you implement these principles, remember something fundamental. It is your development plan; ask for help where you need it, but don't rely on others to make it happen. Once you have committed to your development plan, following it will become more straightforward and purposeful.

Now, let's go back to your professional/career development plan. It's important to note that Key Career Development

Commitments will help you leverage strengths, gain experience, grow, and achieve readiness for the next role.

In this development plan, you must identify the Leadership Competencies needed (Hard and Soft Skills) to intentionally nurture them and be ready when the opportunity shows up. Coach John Wooden said, "*When opportunity comes, it's too late to prepare.*"

If you start learning about Leadership now, not only will you increase your opportunities, but you'll also make the most of them when they arrive. Let me break it down for you.

Hard Skills are specific, teachable tasks that can be defined and measured. Examples include knowing how to navigate Microsoft Office programs, etc.

Soft Skills are behaviors related to how you interact in the workplace. Examples include teamwork, communication, accountability, etc.

Soft skills like communicating and working together are the most sought-after employee skills. 92% of recruiters say soft skills are critical tools they look for in their applicants. However, we know these skills don't come naturally to everyone.

The Top 10 Soft Skills

- *Communication*
- *Self-motivation*
- *Empathy*
- *Responsibility*
- *Team Work*
- *Problem solving*

- *Decisiveness*
- *Ability to Work Under Pressure & Time Management*
- *Flexibility*
- *Negotiation and Conflict Resolution*

Activity:

Here is a quick activity to help you improve your awareness of these soft skills.

Ask three to five people who know you well to rate you from zero to ten in these ten soft skills areas above. Leave a space next to each of them to allow comments with each rating.

You will be surprised how much you'll find out after this. Be open to receiving the feedback and intentional about making some changes as you discover these growth opportunities.

Using the management track as a guidepost is helpful for both the employee and the leader measure progress towards professional goals.

While a set timeline for advancing into management might not be possible, having benchmarks and guideposts along the way keeps you and your leader on the same page in terms of progress.

A Clear Track Ensures Quality Training and Support

"Leaders become great not because of their power but because of their ability to empower others"
— John C. Maxwell

When we talk about transitions, it is vital to remember that a laid-out management track is important when planning training, support, and development.

Being an HR professional, specifically in the Learning and Development space, allows me to understand that it is easier to equip employees with the right tools and training when they have clarity about their goals and where they want to go.

When the front-line staff realizes that the people promoted from within the organization are using the same management track that they are following, it gives them a level of assurance that they will be going through the same (or similar) training and development experiences.

Organizations that make certain types of training or education mandatory for those moving into management, either before they take the position or shortly after, helps ensure consistency of training across management roles.

When the management track is clear, it helps the organization set priorities in allocating proper human and financial resources towards training, development, and other forms of support.

Here is an example of a clear track that ensures quality training and support for a team member.

- First, identify Professional Development Competency like TEAMWORK.
- The next step will be to note the Specific Areas of Focus like ACCOUNTABILITY, COMMUNICATION, or PRESENTING.
- Then lay out a specific Training Plan.

- This final step supports the accountability component, which is to schedule quarterly progress review meetings with your leader or mentor.

People pay attention to what you measure. No one will care about the things not tracked. Remember the three components: Training/Education, Support, and Development.

Succession Planning and Change Management

"A mentor is someone who allows you to see the hope inside yourself" — Unknown

What is succession planning? Succession planning is identifying and internally developing talent to replace key business leadership positions in the organization. It increases the availability of capable individuals prepared to assume leadership roles.

Another way a clear management track can also benefit you as an individual and the organization is in succession planning and managing change.

When employees are on the management track, it is much simpler to determine who might be ready to move into management or higher executive roles, especially those working with mentors.

Mentors can start grooming new managers to take over early on, so succession goes as smoothly as possible. I am someone who has personally benefited from mentorship for many years.

Here are just some of the benefits you can find in mentoring:

- Increases your self-awareness
- It exposes you to new and different perspectives
- You learn from others' experiences
- Improvement in goal-setting

Let's go back to succession planning; If personnel changes are sudden in your organization, you want to be a part of that cohort of new managers in development. You are prepared to step in and assume a vacant position.

A similar scenario happens when organizations grow; they have to create new management positions. In that case, you benefit if you are the furthest along on the management track to fill that role.

A study done by Roy Maurer from SHRM (Society for Human Resource Management) shows that internal mobility boots retention. He found that employees who move around within a company, whether to new jobs in different departments or promotions, are more likely to stay with that company.

This plan helps minimize outside hiring (with all its associated costs) while also ensuring that qualified candidates possess the key competencies to qualify for vacant or new positions. Promoting internal candidates has multiple advantages; one is that the employees are already familiar with organizational culture and resources. May have robust peer networks in place and understand the organization's day-to-day.

Remember these:

Someone Leaves ---> New Managers have been groomed for the position.

Expansion---->Employees from the management track are prepared.

Let me leave you with this last thought. Work hard at what you do, and those around you will see it, and you will gain influence. Why? Remember, you are a leader too, and Leadership is influential and is highly visual; people do what people see. Influence cannot be mandated; you must earn it. You must earn the right to lead others. Don't fall into just being a manager; become a leader.

Practical Illustration

"In the middle of difficulty lies opportunity"
— Albert Einstein

Over the three years, despite the challenges with the pandemic, hotel occupancy has grown tremendously. As the business has expanded, they had to hire nearly a dozen new managers. Almost all of these came from outside the hospitality industry, and the transitions were often challenging.

While these new managers were intelligent and talented, they often did not easily adjust to the culture. The turnover is higher than they would have liked to see among these new managers. "They could not understand why more of their people didn't want to move into management," then they thought. "Maybe they do, but they are not sure how. Maybe we should find a way to make that clearer." Together with a group of high-level managers, they created a clear path to management. Someone in the team created a flow sheet for each division to show potential ways through front-line positions into management. They presented this to their leaders in a webinar and posted it on the intranet. The next time a managerial position was open, they were pleased to see that four internal candidates applied. Each was far enough along on the track to qualify.

CHAPTER 9

READY, SET, EMPOWER

> *"Management isn't some skill like drawing where you can practice in isolation for hours and hours on end. You need to have the opportunity to be stretched in certain situations to learn to grow." — Julio Zhuo*

"I am promoting you to a manager as of today!"

Up until now, I have been swimming in this vast fishbowl within the organization as an individual contributor. Now I am a new manager, and the fear grips me, and doubt creeps in. I am unsure if I can do this? After a couple of weeks, my manager noticed how stressed I was and was kind enough to answer some of my concerns—the beginning of the turnaround in approaching my new job.

Does this sound familiar? As a new manager is natural to feel unsure of yourself. It takes time to gain confidence and to feel empowered.

Empowering employees is a crucial task for new and aspiring leaders alike. As you follow your career journey, consider how you can adapt your leadership style to unlock team members' potential and overcome organizational challenges.

Making Decisions

Sound decision-making can help managers show their employees that you truly value what they do and have their best interest at heart. When managers designate time to evaluate, analyze and explain decisions, they also display consideration and trustworthiness.

A new manager is playing a new game, which is unfamiliar.

In the past, you were a team member, following the traditional ways and answering to management.

Now, you are the leader of the pack. Therefore, it is essential to 'Empower new managers' and encourage them to step up and make decisions confidently.

What is needed to make decisions or guide steps for a new manager?

1. Get a mentor that is willing to be your sounding board for you as you settle into your new role.
2. The mentor must not be a crutch for you, but you must feel their support in your decision-making.

How would you like to be Empowered as a Hesitant Manager?

1. Let the manager make simple, low-risk decisions independently
2. Advance them to make more critical decisions by seeking guidance
3. Wean the new managers from dependence and navigate fully into their role.

4. Encourage levels of trust and avoid overriding a new manager's decision unless the consequences could have damaging results.
5. Support the new manager's decisions with employees.
6. Consult in private with the new manager over any disputes of decisions
7. Maintain regular communications with your up-line manager for input on significant decisions or advice on complex matters.

Asking for Help – Cast a rope of hope to build confidence

"Confidence and empowerment are cousins, in my opinion." — Amy Jo Martin

It is unfair to expect that a new manager will have all the tools in the toolbox.

Are you feeling incompetent and weak at this point? Of course you are!

Therefore, a 'newbie on the block' must feel assured that it is safe to ask for help.

I believe this will, with immediate effect, lower the stress levels and eliminate errors on the job.

So I am suggesting that it is better to ask for help than do something and do it wrong. You don't want to face those consequences because they could be damaging. There is no need to dig a hole and put your head in like an ostrich because of embarrassment.

When I think of myself as an equipping leader, I must introduce my new leader to all I know, help set goals and achieve goals along their journey.

You can begin the process by meeting with your team and asking them questions to gain insights into how to support them.

What questions should a new manager ask his team?

- *How can I be of help to you?*
- *What is your communication style?*
- *How can I make you comfortable when we have a feedback session?*
- *What are you striving for professionally?*
- *What kind of work inspires you?*
- *What are some of your biggest challenges at the moment?*
- *How do you want to be recognized?*

The last thing we want a new manager is to feel bad because they asked for a helping hand.

Support Don't Micromanage

> *"A boss wants to pay for results, and an employee wants recognition for effort. If a boss recognizes effort, they will get even better results."* — Simon Sinek

The new manager will have to learn and make some mistakes. They will need to be supported but don't micromanage or undermine their authority if you are their go-to person.

The challenge is to find the balance between micromanaging and being too hands-off may be a little different for each new manager.

Research shows that micromanagement is among the top three reasons employees resign. It kills creativity, breeds mistrust, causes undue stress, and demoralizes your team.

Beating the Micromanager

If you want to avoid consequences, here are five tips for doing and putting a stop to micromanaging your employees.

1. Highlight Delegating

Give tasks to each team player according to their strengths and goals, and they become equipped and grow. When delegating is not a step-by-step process of completing the project, that's *micromanaging*. Turn the spotlight on the intended outcome and provide them with the right resources, training, and authority to reach the end goal.

2. Make Expectations Clear

Make sure that all expectations are crystal clear from the get-go. Set the team up for success and not for failure. How? Establish clear and achievable goals when you want the project to be finished.

You're telling them *what* you want them to accomplish, not *how* you expect them to achieve it.

3. Who is On the Bus?

You might be saying that is obvious but let me tell you that having the wrong people on the bus will make you micromanage because that person doesn't have the proper skill set or tools in the toolbox.

4. Ditch Perfectionism

I like the way Julia Cameron describes perfectionism;

"Perfectionism doesn't believe in practice shots. It doesn't believe in improvement. Perfectionism has never heard that anything worth doing is worth doing badly and that if we allow ourselves to do something badly, we might in time become quite good at it."

Abort from being old school, we did it this way, and it is how we continue. It is ditching perfectionism not to let your team stagnate but instead embrace and reward creativity with the possibility of failure as your employee's new unchartered waters.

5. Discover How Your Team Desires to Be Managed

I decide I want to have a candid conversation with my team members. I want to know their preferences and determine their expectations of being managed. One might say, *"Please hold my hand,"* and another will value the trust and embrace autonomy. Sound like you?

This two-way dialogue shows your employees that you respect their input and let go of any assumptions you might have about how you're performing as a manager. At this point, you might just be ignoring the signs that you're a micromanager.

Give space to the employees to learn, grow, fail and discover.

Trust their judgment, skills, and expertise. Your job is to have your eye on the big picture, not bogged down, micromanaging, in the details.

Continuous Growth and Development

Let me ask you something, "Does an Olympic athlete stop training after the Olympics?" If you think yes, you are gravely mistaken.

We are like Olympian athletes. It would be best if you grew yourself continuously.

I love what John Maxwell says – "To be effective as a manager, we must raise our lids to lead our teams."

You are a few months into this new role, and you feel that some team members are showing great potential. The light-bulb goes on, and you recognize the need for growth and development.

> *"If you want to lead, you must learn.*
> *If you're going to continue to lead, you must*
> *continue to learn"* — *John C. Maxwell*

Formal management development of on-the-job and off-the-job development includes internal workshops and external training.

Additionally, provide ongoing growth opportunities by delegating extra tasks, which is an advantage to the manager and a chance to evaluate their performance.

John Maxwell's book "Everyone Communicates, Few Connect" is a good start if you want to be effective and learn communication skills.

I cannot agree more with Roddy Galbraith when he said, "It drives me nuts when 'communication' is labeled a SOFT skill. I don't care how good your content is, how great the PowerPoint is, how wonderfully skilled you are technically; communication is one hundred percent an essential key to success."

In everything - job interviews, relationships, management, presentations, brainstorming, networking, and on and on! Your communication is what sets **you** apart!

Through the feedback process, regular check-ins, and employee reviews, the manager continues to identify areas of development. Help them identify ways to build strengths even further and address needed growth.

Conclusion

As I looked back on my career journey, I realized that I had gained valuable help from my supervisors as they empowered me.

My manager...

Delegated effectively *without micromanaging*

Provided the resources *and training needed for me to deliver*

Set clear expectations *to understand the decisions I was empowered to make as the boundaries.*

Coached me *and provided constructive feedback*

Helped me *communicate the company's vision, goals, and culture*

It helped me *build my confidence by demonstrating that the company had faith in my capabilities.*

Empowering Application Exercises:

Are you getting help where you need it?

If not, take some time out and fathom out what you need; new skills, mentoring, coaching. Growth is ongoing. You have to sharpen the knife constantly. Place high priority on investing in the right things to your benefit in the long run.

Are you a continual learner?

A leader must not fall into the massive trap of slacking off when achieving a position.

Rick Warren, the author in Purpose Driven Life, says, *"The moment you stop learning is the moment you stop leading."*

I believe this will help you have a constant appetite for more significant achievements and accomplishments. It will add to your credibility and attract your followers.

Do you have a plan?

You need to know what you plan to do this week, next week, following six months, six months from now, a year from now?

Color-code your calendar. I like to use red; this means can make no changes. Amber means can move this training session to another date. Green means it is essential; however, it can adjust it.

Practical Illustration

Carlos was a star employee when he was a staff accountant. He was decisive and resourceful and had strong problem-solving skills. When he was promoted to Lead Accountant, Carlos thought the same skills would make him succeed in his new role. Boy, was he wrong! He had been with the organization for ten years and felt like he knew all there was to know. During his first month as a Department lead, however, he found himself facing many problems he didn't know how to solve, from balance sheets inconsistencies, missing essential documents, and on top of all of that, personnel conflicts. He was frustrated and worried that he was not cut out for the job. His supervisor, Mario, noticed that Carlos seemed more and more stressed by the day.

"You know, you're not in this alone," Mario told him during their weekly check-in. "It's OK to ask for help.

When I first started as a manager here, I called HR almost every day with a question!"

Carlos was surprised – Mario seemed to have it all together.

He told Carlos a bit about the problems he faced early in his leadership career. Mario gave him the phone numbers and email addresses of two people, whom Carlos should have on speed dial and help him when needed.

Carlos left the meeting feeling much less stressed and much more comfortable with the idea of asking for help.

CHAPTER 10

YOU OWN YOUR GROWTH

"Growth is the best separator between those who succeed and those who do not." — John C. Maxwell

Next Level Growth Strategies for going from a New Manager to a Great Leader

Being a new manager is tough. During a rotational assignment, I woke up one day, went to work, and my boss and mentor called me into the office and said, "starting next week, I would like you to manage a new department created at the direction of the Board." No pressure, right! And, just like that, I was a new Senior Manager. This promotion was an exciting time in my career.

I feel fortunate that the company invested in my professional growth before this progression, including on-the-job experience, developing core leadership competencies, targeted education & training programs, high-exposure assignments, and relationship building. But, managing peers, more experienced employees, and high-profile projects for executives/stakeholders without specific experience or training was a significant challenge.

Managing people is a complex and essential enterprise. Suppose you are transitioning to a leader of people. In that case, you might also feel ill-prepared, ill-equipped, isolated, and afraid of making mistakes—you might even think, as I did, that failure is not an option. I realize that helping new managers succeed does not have to be a great mystery. We will look at approaches and strategies that have proven successful over my career and reinforced by studies.

Organizations are looking for employees who can grow into new management positions or leadership roles in the future. Employees are looking for organizations that value growth. New managers must meet the needs and expectations of a diverse and dynamic workforce. They must serve as coaches and mentors, be accessible and communicate effectively. Some organizations expect a new manager to hit the ground running with the needed expertise, but that is simply untrue, judging from my career journey.

- According to an article from the Center for Creative Leadership (Set Your New Managers Up for Success | Developing New Leaders | CCL):
- According to their subordinates, twenty percent of first-time managers are doing a poor job.
- Twenty-six percent of first-time managers felt they were not ready to lead others.
- Sixty percent of first-time managers said they never received any training when transitioning into their first leadership role.

"Based on our decades of research and experience developing first-level managers, the Center for Creative Leadership suggests three things to increase their chances of success."

- Clarify the challenges of shifting from individual contributor to manager.

- Provide new managers with the knowledge and practical tools.
- Create continuity in learning.

Developing managers into leaders is more critical than ever. In the book "The 15 Invaluable Laws of Growth" by my mentor and thought leader John C. Maxwell wrote, "The Law of Intentionality says that growth does not just happen. You must be intentional about your growth."

According to a Hay Group study (Identifies Best Companies for Leadership), the best companies for leadership take a determined and intentional approach to help leaders develop and rise within their organization.

We never stop growing. Even when an employee has grown into a management position, the development process must continue. Employees who feel they cannot grow in their current job or organization are likely unhappy and may not stay. New managers need to gain experience and develop within their managerial role, whether to eventually move into even higher positions or become more skilled at managing. Continue to challenge new managers to grow, strengthen their current skills, and develop new ones that will benefit the individual managers and the organization.

"The conventional definition of management is getting work done through people, but natural management develops people through work" — Agha Hasan Abedi

Seek Continuous Growth Opportunities

As a John Maxwell Coach, we believe that reaching your potential is a constant journey of discovery, growth, and insight, which requires curiosity, consistency, and willingness to change. Great organizations place a high priority on their employees' continuous learning and development. Developing a new manager does not end when they assume the managerial role. No matter your industry or role, there is always room to grow. Growth and development involve the process of improving or expanding an employee's skills set to achieve specific goals. These objectives may include a promotion, lateral moves, or ownership of a high-profile project. Whether an employee wants to move into upper management or another position eventually or make the most of their current managerial position, it is vital to find ways for new managers to grow continuously. Work with individual new managers to explore the areas they would like to grow.

In an Annual Leadership Development Survey Report for Training Magazine, organizations prioritized the following Leadership Skills:

- Coaching and communication
- Diversity and Inclusion
- Interpersonal relationship skills
- Motivating others and taking accountability.

When a new manager expresses interest in building leadership skills, work with them to find opportunities. Growth opportunities might include:

- Taking courses outside of work.
- Completing internal training.
- Working with others on a unique project or committee.

Empower your new managers to take charge of their growth and development. Also, be sure that new managers know the organization's growth opportunities, such as workshops, committees, projects, or special initiatives. If you hear of a possibility that seems a good fit for one of your new managers, bring it to their attention. Encourage new managers to be alert for growth opportunities and discuss possibilities with you.

Create a Development Plan

"If you go to work on your goals, your goals will go to work on your plan, and your plan will go to work on you. Whatever good things we build end up building us."
— Jim Rohn

If you want to have a fulfilling and thriving career, taking charge of your growth strategy is essential. The critical steps to career growth opportunities at your company are knowing what you want to be doing in five or ten years, setting clear goals, putting a plan in place, and communicating with your manager. All new managers are encouraged to set "stretch goals" which are challenging and push them to exceed expectations.

Great Leaders conduct performance reviews, encourage ongoing coaching conversations through one-on-one meetings to ensure goals are on track, feedback is given and received, and new managers have the support and resources needed for success.

The personal development plan helps the new manager shape the next phase of their career. Having a clear development plan helps the new manager clarify their goals and the steps towards them and enables supervisors to best support new managers.

Provide Regular Feedback

As a new manager, I often took feedback personally. Regular feedback is essential in the development of any employee, and especially in developing new managers. Feedback is a gift. Take the time to provide regular feedback, both positive and developmental, to new managers. Ensure that you take the time to ask them for feedback, as they may not approach you with concerns or questions. When a new manager first assumes a management role, it is clever to schedule regular one-on-one meetings, check-ins, or feedback sessions, as often as once a week.

My company conducted 360-degree surveys to understand how managers, peers, customers, and team members perceived new managers. Through this process, I learned that I was perceived as micro-managing, failing to delegate, and causing stress for the team. Also, take opportunities to give feedback on projects or anything else you observe. Do not just give feedback when you see something go wrong or notice a development need. Be sure to provide positive, affirming feedback when things are going well. When new managers only receive developmental feedback, they may feel they can do nothing right. Take the time to acknowledge growth, improvement, and work done well.

Embrace a Mentoring Culture

When you have a great mentor, it can be one of the most powerful relationships in your career. Becoming a mentor to others is also rewarding. Mentoring is a beautiful way to keep employees learning and growing. We strongly encourage mentoring at all levels of an organization. This critical relationship-building and exposure activity can be formal or informal programs. We encourage new managers to continue collaborating with past mentors and encourage mentors to continue finding ways to help their mentees grow. If a new manager wishes to develop a particular skill or explore a unique management aspect, encourage them to find a skilled mentor in this area. As a new manager, working one-on-one with a mentor provides a chance to learn new skills, strengthen existing ones, and build professional relationships and networks. Finally, encourage new managers to become mentors to their employees and to those who wish to enter management in the future. By becoming mentors themselves, new managers have a chance to build skills in building talent and invest in their people. Mentoring relationships are crucial components of career development planning and performance review.

Practical Illustration

Non-Profit Organizations Promote Mentoring and Growth Opportunities.

"As we look ahead into the next century,
leaders will be those who empower others."
— Bill Gates

James is enthusiastic about empowering communities, changing lives through arts and culture, and impacting the next generation of leaders. A mentor inspired James to advance to the level of having a corner office with lots of windows. This visual empowered him to see the "Big Picture" of what was possible for his career as a leader. One of his proudest moments was hiring a former mentee' as his Grants Manager. James attributes his success to the mentors who provided guidance, advice, and a bigger vision for his future. Today, we find James in his corner office with big windows overlooking the city and allowing a first-year high school student to shadow him at work. His organization builds a stronger community through the arts by paying it forward, which he gained through mentorship, coaching, and leadership development. His organization provides growth opportunities to non-profit directors and flexible scheduling/funding for his staff to pursue training and development.

Adopt a Coaching Style to Managing

I obtained a coaching certification to help provide business coaching and mentoring to diverse suppliers in the Utility Industry. As a Certified Sherpa Executive Coach, we define coaching as a form of development usually based on one-on-one discussions, providing guidance and advice for specific challenges/behaviors that new managers encounter. Successful organizations use coaching discussions to help emerging leaders address their fears and developmental areas. Having a coach and mentor available was extremely helpful to my career and success as a new manager. While a mentor and a coach are two distinct roles, they share some characteristics that benefit the new manager, such as giving career advice and offering help when needed. Tools are available to help coach and mentor any new manager, including performance reviews, feedback, and open communication.

As the Chinese Proverb says, "Give a man a fish, and you feed him for a day. Teach a man to fish, and you feed him for a lifetime".

Conclusion

> *"There is no passion for being found playing small and settling for a life that is less than the one you are capable of living."* — Nelson Mandela

I have been studying leadership and personal growth for over 30 years. I am still finding new ways to grow and improve as an entrepreneur. John Maxwell's teachings have demonstrated that to reach your potential, you must do more than go through life hoping for the best—you must seize growth opportunities as if your future depends on it. As you move forward in an organization, remember that great organizations prioritize growth and development, and great leaders are lifelong learners. I think of my growth journey as a long-country mile from struggle to success and finally striving to leave a legacy of significance. Maya Angelo said it best, "Success is liking yourself, liking what you do, and liking how you do it."

Are you ready to get started?

Let's Begin Your Growth Journey

"In every business, in every industry, management does matter." — *Michael Eisner*

How far you grow as a leader is truly up to you, but following the strategies in this book could be the first step you need to bridge the gap between where you are and where you want to be. Here is a summary of key actions you can take to accelerate your personal leadership growth and development:

- Set challenging "stretch" goals
- Use an Individual Development Plan and formal assessments to increase self-awareness and assess leadership strengths/personality
- Participate in external Leadership Development Programs or Professional certification Programs
- Become a Mentor or Mentee
- Accept rotational assignments and roles in different departments/cross-functional teams
- Hire a Coach
- Practice a Coaching Management Style
- Develop Relationships Internally and Externally
- Seek High-Profile Exposure to Stakeholders/Executives
- Be patient, learn from your mistakes, and most of all, Believe You Can Do This!

Practical Illustration

Executive Perspective

Organizational commitment and engagement in leadership growth and development positively impact business results. During my career, one of the most impactful Executives demonstrated key strategies that impacted business outcomes during his tenure as Vice President in the Utility Industry. Russ summed up his approach as a Servant Leader in three words: "Intentional, consistent, and determined."

He was always intentional about growth and consistently invested in providing growth opportunities to high performers in the organization. He was determined to hold himself and his leadership team accountable for the teams' success. After inquiring about my goals during our first briefing meeting, he elevated my Supplier Diversity function, expanded my responsibilities, and consistently offered stretch assignments, feedback, and coaching. Russ intentionally leads by example. He is still determined to impact the next generation of leaders through consultant projects, volunteer teaching activities, and mentoring students through job shadowing.

NOTES

Chapter 3- Define and Build Competencies

1. The Life Sciences Trainers & Educators Network (LTEN) website. Take the Quiz: What's Your Potential to Be an Empowering .... https://www.l-ten.org/bonus-focus/take-the-quiz-whats-your-potential-to-be-an-empowering-leader/
2. PPT - Developing New Managers Corporate Training Materials ....
3. https://www.slideserve.com/garyleonard/developing-new-managers-corporate-training-materials-powerpoint-ppt-presentation
4. Your Road Map for Success (Versão em Inglês) Resumo https://www.getabstract.com/pt/resumo/your-road-map-for-success/7986
5. Key Questions to Uncover Your Strengths. https://www.burrisinstitute.com/blogs/Key-Questions-to-Uncover-Your-Strengths
6. The 21 Indispensable Qualities of a Leader. https://www.time-management-central.net/support-files/the-21-qualities-summary.pdf

Chapter 5- Provide Effective Tools

7. THE 21 IRREFUTABLE LAWS OF LEADERSHIP. http://cdn1.johnmaxwellteam.com/cds/10in10/Attachments/90Day21LawsPersonalStoryWorksheet.pdf
8. 100 Ways to Motivate Others by Steve Chandler & Scott Richardson

Chapter 7- Identify Strong Candidates Early

9. NFL Pro Bowl https://www.sbnation.com/nfl-pro-bowl
10. We Wait Too Long to Train Our Leaders by Jack Zenger https://hbr.org/2012/12/why-do-we-wait-so-long-to-trai
11. https://www.forbes.com/sites/forbescoachescouncil/2019/10/24/lack-of-trust-can-make-workplaces-sick-and-dysfunctional/?sh=52a1940c44d1
12. Knute Rockne - The secret is to work less as individuals... https://www.brainyquote.com/quotes/knute_rockne_390851
13. Why you're waiting far too long to begin leadership .... https://www.mbassett.com/blog/why-youre-waiting-far-too-long-to-begin-leadership-development
14. Gallup Report: How Millennials Want to Work and Live. Purpose • Development • Coach • Ongoing Conversations • Strengths • Life THE SIX BIG CHANGES LEADERS HAVE TO MAKE 2016

Chapter 8- Clearly Define The Management Track

15. Getting career clarity is asking yourself the right .... https://strengthsdrivencareer.com/getting-career-clarity/
16. Questions You Should Ask Yourself Before Accepting a Job .... https://www.biospace.com/article/questions-you-should-ask-yourself-before-accepting-a-job-offer/
17. Nine key soft skills to develop in teens | Cyprus Mail. https://cyprus-mail.com/2021/06/22/nine-key-soft-skills-to-develop-in-teens/
18. Why Mentoring Matters. "A mentor is someone who allows you https://medium.com/joinwest/why-mentoring-matters-ec54cfdb828b

Chapter 10- You Own Your Growth

19. Set Your New Managers Up for Success | Developing New Leaders | CCL article https://www.ccl.org/articles/leading-effectively-articles/prepare-first-time-leaders-success/

20. Eighth Annual Hay Group Study Identifies Best Companies for Leadership | The HR Gazette (hr-gazette.com https://hr-gazette.com/eighth-annu-al-hay-group-study-identifies-best-companies-for-leader-ship/#:~:text=Eighth%20Annual%20Hay%20Group%20Study%20Identifies%20Best%20Companies,%2048%20percent%20%2017%20more%20rows%20

21. Annual Leadership Development Survey: Developing the Hearts and Minds of Leaders (trainingmag.com) https://trainingmag.com/annual-leadership-development-survey-developing-the-hearts-and-minds-of-leaders/

22. Weyerhaeuser. Growth and Development. https://www.weyerhaeuser.com/careers/what-we-offer/growth-and-development/

MEET THE AUTHORS

CEDRICK LAFLEUR

Cedrick LaFleur is a motivational and empowering Senior Executive with more than 30 years of success across the healthcare sales, leadership, and sports industries. Cedrick has been married to Tammie for 35 years, they have 2 children, TreKessa (35 yrs old) and Patrick (30 yrs old).

Cedrick is the Founder and Chief Executive at LaFleur Leadership Institute, which focuses on building best-in-class leaders, keynote speaking and training.

Cedrick is an Executive Director with John Maxwell Team. He is also a Dave Ramsey certified Master Financial Coach.

Cedrick is the Chairman of the Executive Leadership Circle, which is a private organization where thought leaders discuss and address global topics. Finally, he serves as Founding Partner and President of Lake Charles Education Collaboration, Inc. a 501c3 Education Based Think Tank.

Cedrick recently retired as Regional Sales Manager, from Abbott Laboratories after serving for 22 years.

Contact info:
E-Mail: cedrick.lafleur2@gmail.com
Website: www.lafleurleadershipinstitute.com

DENEEN HUMPHREY

"It's a great day to be great" is the adopted mantra that you will hear whenever you are speaking with Deneen R. Humphrey, the CEO of The D.R. Humphrey Group and Founder of A Greater Glory Ministries. With more than 30 years of bi-vocational experience, Deneen brings a "can do" approach to every opportunity and to every obstacle. Being the divorced mother of two adult daughters, Deneen is proof positive that success may come in various forms, but at the end of it all, you will find her declaring "it's all good because it's all God. Visit her at http://www.drhumphreygroup.com for more information.

TYWAUNA WILSON, MBA, MLS (ASCP)^{CM}

Tywauna Wilson, MBA, MLS(ASCP) CM, is a leadership innovator, medical laboratory scientist, speaker, author, podcast host, and career coach who helps professionals unleash their star power to advance in their careers by growing their leadership, increasing their influence, and multiplying their impact. Her mission is "to empower and train one million leaders to be able to lead with confidence and leave a legacy that makes them proud."

She is a graduate of Kentucky State and Indiana Wesleyan universities where she received her Bachelor of Science in clinical laboratory science and MBA, respectively. Ms. Wilson has nearly 20 years of diverse medical laboratory and progressive healthcare leadership experience. She is viewed as a leadership innovator in the medical laboratory community and has received several accolades in the past year including: 2021 ASCP Career Ambassador Award and 2021 Cardinal Health™ Laboratory Excellence List Advocacy Winner.

Ms. Wilson is the founder of Trendy Elite Coaching and Consulting, which develops best-in-class leaders through its Standout Leader Academy, coaching, and leadership training programs. She is also an Executive Director with the John Maxwell Team. Ms. Wilson is the author of the book, Some Leaders Wear Lab Coats, the author of Leadership Tidbits®, a series of personal growth books, and host of the "eLABorate Topics," and "Leadership Tidbits® with Coach Tee Wilson" podcasts. Ms. Wilson is active in her community and enjoys advocating for medical laboratory professionals and emerging leaders. In addition to her professional endeavors, she considers her "most important titles are that of being a wife and mom." Visit her at https://tywaunawilson.com for more information.

DARLENE GLENN

Welcome, I'm Darlene Glenn from Atlanta, GA. As a small business owner, I spent the first part of my career in sales with a Fortune 50 company. Then, in Corporate America as a Business Consultant and Senior Sales Manager. In 2018 I became a certified John Maxwell speaker, trainer, and coach. My professional background, the John Maxwell Team resources, and the certification in human behavior analysis have created an all-inclusive set of tools that can be uniquely designed for each organization's exclusive needs. I am the Founder and Chief Inspiration Officer of Aspire Lighthouse Leadership, where we help people Ignite Growth and become Rock Solid.

My mission is to empower my clients with the necessary tools to enhance their self-awareness, self-confidence, leadership influence, and productivity while bringing balance to their lives. My greatest passion is helping others recognize their unique potential by unlocking their blindness to see their greatness. The journey to significance begins with intentional living, one step at a time, day after day. It is in being that one becomes their best self. Visit her at www.darleneglenn.com.

PAULETHA WHITE

Pauletha White is the Founder and Executive Director of K.I.N.D. Girls Mentoring Program ["Knowledge Influencing Noble Decisions"], the platform where she discovered her voice. Her greatest passion is bringing leadership and vision to our society – especially girls. One of the ways she empowers youth is by showing them that they can think, feel, and choose even in our modern technological culture. The practical keys that are taught give girls the blueprint of a balanced woman. They can apply them to their lives in making the right choices and becoming successful in life. Each individual process information differently, which is why these keys are presented in a fun and interactive manner challenging youth to think independently, research, ask questions, and discover solutions. She strongly believes that students can become authentic leaders and rise to the challenges the emerging generation will face. A suitable place to start developing these critical leadership skills is within middle and high school students already exhibiting an interest in leadership.

Pauletha is also a member of the John Maxwell Team and a certified Personal Development coach. "Leaders cannot give what they do not have." It is crucial to discover who you are at the core, have a personal plan on how you are going to intentionally grow, and choose the right path. She will continue to add value to her staff and leaders of all ages by teaching leaderships principles and strategies to release their passion and reach their best potential in life. Visit her at www.thepathforleaders.com for more information

JOHANNA RINCON

Johanna Rincon is a mother, wife, entrepreneur, and self-motivated woman who enjoys personal growth and adding value to others.

She Equips, Inspires, and Empowers individuals to be the best version of themselves. She accomplished this by facilitating Personal Growth, Leadership Development, Personal Values training, Coaching, and Mentoring sessions.

CEO of Internal Alignment LLC. Born and raised in the Dominican Republic, she came to the US when she was 14 years old and did not speak a word of English. Despite all the difficult circumstances, she is very grateful for her family. She married Freddy Alexis Rincon, and together they have their two daughters, Alexa and Alianna, who are her inspiration.

Johanna also serves in the capacity of Leadership Success Coach in Newark Alliance with the Newark 2020 Hiring Initiative. A career in the Hospitality industry for 18 years and 15 of those have been with the Four Seasons Hotels.

Certified Coach, Speaker & Trainer with The John Maxwell Team. Certified Human Behavior Consultant (DISC) and Maxwell Certified Parenting and Family Coach.

DEBBIE REID

Ms. Reid was born and raised in Port Elizabeth, South Africa, now residing in Seoul, South Korea.

Debbie has dedicated herself to developing and motivating people for the past 30 years in business and the sporting arena.

Before moving to Seoul, Debbie was the founder and owner of Zoom Sportswear.

She became a Maxwell Certified Leadership Coach, Trainer, Speaker, and Personality and Behavioral Analysis. (DISC)

Her 18 years of residency in Korea has developed her career as a Communication Coach for C level in large, small, and medium-sized companies. She specializes in teaching and coaching clients and has a presence in front of different types of audiences.

Debbie is also a motivational trainer who can awaken people's potential, leadership, and integrity.

Debbie has facilitated communication workshops and offered coaching services for numerous clients, including developing leaders, CEOs, and Christian leaders.

She believes that her purpose is to connect people, help them to recognize their purpose to be different, and live an empowered life.

ELLA L. CLARK, CPCC, CSC

Ella Clark is a certified executive coach, trainer and speaker with The John Maxwell Team and Sherpa Coaching, Inc., who has devoted more than 30 years to developing leaders and organizations. After serving as a successful leader with a major corporation, she founded the Clark Group LLC. As a certified Minority Business Enterprise, the company specializes in helping individuals and organizations become more effective at achieving their highest potential and purpose. Ella partners with community organizations to support, empower and accelerate opportunities for under-resourced youth, adults, and people with disabilities.

Before launching The Clark Group, LLC, Ella was the manager of supplier and partner initiatives at the Tennessee Valley Authority. She provided coaching, consulting, advocacy, and oversight of the agency's efforts to advance small businesses. During her professional career, she has held increasingly challenging leadership roles in minority economic development, marketing, customer service, sales, education, training, diversity

& inclusion, and supplier diversity. She lives in Chattanooga, Tennessee. Visit her at www.clarkgroupcoaching.com.

THANK YOU

Thank you for reading Rise Up: The Blueprint For Manager Success.

Leave Us A Review:

If you were able to learn and grow from this book, please take a moment to write a review as your words truly make a difference. Book Reviews can be done on Amazon.com, or you can send us an e-mail at Cedrick.lafleur2@gmail.com with the subject line "Review."

Need Additional Leadership Mentoring Or Coaching:

We exist to help build best-in-class leaders and to help you or your organization improve your market momentum. We exist to help your team deliver outstanding customer experiences. For training, keynotes, workshops, or one-on-one coaching. Please visit www.lafleurleadershipinstitute.com

For Executive Coaching visit: www.grind365series.com

For Online Training:

Want to provide your team with an online training suite of tools and training. With over 150 online courses, we can help you and your team continually grow and develop. Visit www. lafleurleadershipinstitute.com/lms-courses to schedule a call with one of our counselors to discuss your needs.

Made in the USA
Middletown, DE
04 June 2022